Adventures with

APPLES AND SNAKES

From The Garden of Eden

By

George M. Goodrich

authorHOUSE®

AuthorHouse™
1663 Liberty Drive
Bloomington, IN 47403
www.authorhouse.com
Phone: 1-800-839-8640

© 2010 George M. Goodrich. All rights reserved.

No part of this book may be reproduced, stored in a retrieval system, or transmitted by any means without the written permission of the author.

First published by AuthorHouse 7/19/2010

ISBN: 978-1-4520-2844-6 (e)
ISBN: 978-1-4520-2843-9 (sc)
ISBN: 978-1-4520-2842-2 (hc)

Library of Congress Control Number: 2010907890

Printed in the United States of America
Bloomington, Indiana

This book is printed on acid-free paper.

ACKNOWLEDGEMENTS

Jim Munro is a great friend who has challenged me with his great questions during our time together studying the <u>Purpose Driven Life</u>, by Rick Warren and other small group studies. Since these studies were so productive, Jim and George developed questions that occurred because of Eve's encounter with the snake and the apple. These questions eventually served as the chapter titles for this book. Originally, we were to write the book cooperatively. However, it ended that I wrote the book except for Chapter 7, and Jim wrote the discussion questions (except for Chapter 8). We especially appreciate the guidance and input from Bill Sanders, a mutual pastor friend that Jim and I had when Bill was pastor at Buchanan Methodist Church, Buchanan, Michigan, and from Keith Foisy, pastor at Evergreen Evangelical Church in Branch, Michigan. The special English talents of my cousin, Gail Pavlovlich, and a new acquaintance, Rene VanDyke, were gratefully appreciated with all of the editing they performed. I especially want to thank my wife, Sandra Lee, for all of the encouragement she provided and the challenge of commenting on the chapters as they were written. Every one needs a push now and then.

DEDICATION

This book is dedicated to my family; my wife, Sandra Lee, my children Michael Goodrich, David Goodrich and Adona Homminga for all of the time they spent at my side praying and helping as I recovered from legionella.

Table of Contents

Acknowledgements — v
Dedication — vii
Introduction — xi

The Original Sin
Chapter 1 Who Did God Think He Was Any Way? 1
Chapter 2 Wouldn't You Rather Have God Take The Consequences? 9

The Snake
Chapter 3 How Did The Snake Get So Smart? 19
Chapter 4 What Was in It for the Snake? 27
Chapter 5 What Good Is Deception Without Someone To Deceive? 33
Chapter 6 Vertebrate Or Invertebrate? Are You Standing Or Slithering? 41
Chapter 7 To Bite Or Not To Bite, That Is The Question! What Is It About Temptation? 49

The Apple
Chapter 8 Can You Pick A Color….Any Color? Are You A Red Or A Golden Delicious, Or A Sour Granny Smith? 57
Chapter 9 How Big Of A Bite Can You Take? 63

The Knowledge
Chapter 10 Can You Imagine What It Would Have Been Like (If Eve Hadn't Eaten The Apple)? 69
Chapter 11 How Much Knowledge (Good and Evil) Is There? 77
Chapter 12 How Can We Possibly Think That We Can Know As Much As The Creator? 83
Chapter 13 Why Isn't Having All Of This Knowledge Cracked Up To What It Is Supposed To Be? 93
Chapter 14 Does All This Knowledge of Good and Evil Make Us Think We Are God? 101

The Consequences

Chapter 15 Now That You Are On Your Own, What Are You Going To Do? 107

Chapter 16 What's Up With Your Neighbor? Having Trouble Keeping Up With The Joneses? 115

Chapter 17 Which Way Do I Go? Is My G.P.S. Working? 123

Chapter 18 Who's Afraid Of The Big Bad Wolf? Who Turned Out The Lights? 131

Chapter 19 What Is Your Problem? Who Am I Hurting? 139

Chapter 20 Who Is That In The Mirror On The Wall? Is It Me? 147

Chapter 21 Am I Good Or What? It Is All About Me, Isn't It? Is This All For Me? 155

Chapter 22 Can I Get A Drink Around Here? Is It Too Much To Ask To Get Something To Eat? 163

The Final Sacrifice

Chapter 23 Did Mary Really Know The Little Lamb? What Really Happened To The Flock? 171

Chapter 24 Can You Imagine Getting Up In The Morning With Nothing To Work For? 179

Chapter 25 Who Needs Salvation Anyway? We Have An Army For That Don't We? 187

INTRODUCTION

The nature of my occupation as a forensic metallurgical engineer skilled in metal failure analysis often has me in trouble with my ability to critically analyze many given situations. This trait gets me into particular difficulty with normal everyday life where the need for critical assessment is unnecessary and counterproductive. It especially causes difficulty with my wife and friends. Even with this innate desire for saying what I mean and meaning what I say, I find that I can not always accomplish the task. I also find, however, that my ability to critically evaluate cause and effect results in consternation for lawyers (to my delight) when I am in a deposition or on the witness stand. Still, when the lawyers find a hole in my ability to describe what happened, they have the ability to dig the hole deeper to frustrate me.

Knowledge of good and evil is far more reaching than simply lying or cheating. The knowledge of good and evil also includes manipulation, and exploiting, and otherwise taking advantage of situations and opportunities for personal gain. We all know this! Golly, I don't need to write an expose` or a book to teach anyone something new about how to use the knowledge of good and evil to advantage. What I do need to do is convince others that all of us know the difference and that none of us can get away with it. We may think that we are subtle enough to "get one past the other guy", but in reality, the "other guy" is as much aware of what is happening as we are. In fact, the other guy may be allowing it to happen because he feels sorry for the manipulator. Or even worse, the other guy sees an opportunity to double up and get one back. I think that is why we enjoy the movies where we root for the underdog or take delight in the "Sting", or "Oceans Eleven", or "Oceans Thirteen", or what ever number it is up to.

Good and evil knowledge isn't limited to criminals. It isn't limited to hucksters. It isn't limited to schemers. Good and evil knowledge has no limitations of magnitude either. As a matter of fact, we are all guilty of using this knowledge to our advantage in our everyday interchange with our fellow man. Our very existence depends on the fact that knowledge of good and evil is present all around us. We hope that the "good" knowledge rather than the "evil" knowledge prevails. But, we always have our antennas out to be certain that we are not being "used" by someone that is evil driven.

Just in case you haven't thought about it, there is no such thing as a little evil. And in the same manner, there is no such thing as a little good. Even more, there is no such thing as good evil and there is no such thing as evil good. Just to make certain we understand, big evil and big good don't exist either. Evil is evil and good is good **period**! Knowledge of good and evil means all knowledge of good and evil. We can't pretend we don't know the difference! Although some might argue that choosing the lesser evil is acceptable and that the end justifies the means, in my opinion, these arguments are only justifications. They are crutches. Don't buy in on these arguments. Look for the good no matter what!

THE ORIGINAL SIN

CHAPTER 1

Who Did God Think He Was Any Way?

Curiosity, they say, killed the cat.
So what can you do with God's act?

In the beginning, God created heaven and earth[1]. Then He created us! That is when His troubles began, and ours too, I suppose. This book could have started with "Once upon a time there was God. What happened to him any way?" We have kept Him pretty busy with our many demands. Yet, He is still there and He hasn't given up. He wants us to honor Him and He wants us to accept His unconditional love. Somehow, accepting His unconditional love seems to be the problem. Why do we insist on putting conditions on this gift? How can God create something in His own image and expect the creation not to be curious?

Look at how often He has tried to teach us that His love is unconditional. The last time He tried, was when Christ died on the cross and went to hell for us. The time before that, He selected the Israelites to demonstrate how the unconditional love really works. And the time before that, He gave us the gift of "freedom of choice". He tries everyday in some way, but we always manage to muck it up with the choices we make and the consequences we pay. Some choices are good choices. Some choices aren't so good. God has taught and taught and taught! Even so, along comes the snake and we just can't seem to resist that apple.

The Bible has two creation accounts. In the first account, Genesis 1:1 – 2:4 God created the heavens and the earth, Genesis 2:4. In the second account, God created the earth and the heavens, Genesis 2:5. This book is about the second story in Genesis[2]; specifically the Garden of Eden Story. However, even this story has many lessons. There is a lesson about curiosity. There is a lesson about temptation. There is a lesson about making choices and there is a lesson about paying the consequences. All of these lessons have interesting aspects that I will explore with you. But first, consider the beginning of the story.

God created man and then He created woman. They lived a perfect life in the garden and they had a perfect relationship with God. At least, the beginning of the story would lead us to believe that a perfect unblemished relationship existed between God the creator and the humans He created. The story doesn't embellish that part of the relationship to a great extent. However, the implications of the story can certainly be imagined beyond what is stated.

Genesis, Chapter 2, says that mankind had it made. Genesis Chapter 1 says that God was really proud of His creation. This pride can still be seen in Chapter 2 when he gave man the honor of naming all of the animals and birds and was given a mate so that mankind could multiply. (Just for the record, I think that God is still proud of His creation.) Then, in Genesis Chapter 3, along came the snake. Even in the beginning, God told man about the wonders that existed. He told His first creation that they had the run of the garden. The garden had many trees growing from the ground and in the center of the garden He had two special trees, the tree of life and the tree of knowledge of good and evil. He told them they could eat the fruit from any of the trees EXCEPT the tree of knowledge of good and evil. There it is! That tree! The quest was on! The tree of "knowledge" of good and evil that makes us all act stupid! Stupid tree of knowledge any way! Why didn't God just call this the tree of temptation? Why did God have to put it there and then why did He have to tell His creation that it was forbidden? God, what were You thinking? Right in the middle of perfection, He sticks a tree that He doesn't want man to enjoy like the other trees. What was God thinking? God tells these two people He created that if they eat from this tree they will surely die[3]. What was God thinking?

The message I hear from all of this is that He creates all of these "things" and then He tells me that I can enjoy them all. I don't know about you, but this tells me that I live in a perfect world! How much stuff do you have? I know I have a lot. But, there is that stupid tree of knowledge of good and evil beckoning me to want even more. Now, because of that tree, I have knowledge of good and evil along with all of my "stuff". Not only that, I know, if it wasn't for that snake, I could have had all of my "stuff" and not feel guilty about it. Stupid snake anyway. We had it all at the beginning, perfection; yet, we were afraid we were going to miss out on something. Stupid snake; stupid tree, indeed!

When God created mankind, what were His original intentions? What was the purpose that He had in store for us? We can't help but wonder if we existed as creatures that were to serve His special interest whatever they were to be. After all, He had us name all of the animals and the birds and all of the flowers and the trees. Everything was going along just fine! What happened any way? Why did He ever put a temptation in front of us and challenge us to enjoy everything else? He created us in His own image. So, He knew what curiosity was. He knew that we would be curious too. He expected us to ignore the forbidden fruit. You have got to be kidding! Really, did we ever have a choice? The fruit was there. God told us it was there. No way was it going to be ignored, and it wasn't!

The lessons from Rick Warren in his "Purpose Driven Life"[4] are that our purpose is solely for the glory of God. Living with that purpose as a goal in everything we do creates an interesting challenge. Do we try to rationalize the things that we do are for His glory? Do we follow the temptation trail and rationalize that God our creator created the temptation and therefore following the temptation is in His glory? Of course we do! We rationalize everything so that in our minds no matter what we do it is all right with God. I will bet that even Adam and Eve rationalized that eating the fruit would somehow glorify God. However, we also know that we have been taught certain principles, so our rationalization oftentimes is far from what the love and glory of God originally intended.

Still, what were God's original intentions? Were we to be the epitome of devotion? Were we to be contented souls dedicated to putting God on a pedestal in front of everything we did? Were we to be content setting around with bovine placidity toward any and all events? How can God create us in His own image and expect us to sit around lacking curiosity like the story of the original sin would have us believe.

God doesn't need to be set on a pedestal. He is already where He wants to be. After all, He is the Creator. There is nothing, absolutely nothing that we can do to change God. He already told us that "He is" when He told us His name is "I Am"[5]. So why do we keep trying to create God to meet our needs? I think we have lost track of who created whom. Let's face facts; He is not the one that needs to change. Maybe God's motivation is to persuade us that He is all that there is, pantheism, or maybe His motivation is to teach us that He is the center of all motivation; I don't really intend to get in the middle of these issues.

I like the notion that the Garden of Eden story within Genesis was intended to teach us that God has given us the freedom of choice, but like all freedoms, it comes with a price. The price is to protect the freedom while maintaining an acceptable relationship with God. Regardless of what we think, God is the only judge of what is acceptable. To make this relationship acceptable a set of principles exists that seemingly no one can live up to 100% of the time. God showed us in the original story that unimaginable consequences can result if we don't maintain the right relationship with God. In fact, He promised death if we were ever to eat the fruit of the tree that represented good and evil. But then He said in essence," If you want to do it your way, go ahead. Just remember, I am still God, and you are my creation. I still make the rules and the consequences. Glorify Me in all that you do, that is all I ask."[6]

So, here we are still wondering how our curiosity got us into so much trouble. Who did God think He was, any way? He giveth and He taketh away. He tells us "Don't" and lets us do it anyway. When we do what he forbids us to do, He comes crashing down on us. We are what God made us: loving, obedient, faithful, sneaking, hateful, and disobedient. Perfectly created, we may have been, but perfectly behaved, we are not. Although, we had a chance to be perfect, we screwed it up because we wanted to be like God, and know it all. You know what, I can't think of anything that is wrong with that!

Who did God think we were going to be? If we did not have knowledge of "good and evil", what were we supposed to be? How were we supposed to act? How were we supposed to live? What were we supposed to do? What would life be like without good and evil? I guess we were just supposed to enjoy being God's creation! Let's try to imagine life without knowing the difference between good and evil and without being drawn toward one or the other or both.

Without knowledge of good and evil, would we know anything except God's love? Would we know how to take care of ourselves? We probably would not have any reason to distrust anyone. We would not have any desire to out smart anyone. We certainly would not have any wants, because we would not know about other possibilities. We certainly wouldn't be self-seeking. We would not make anything more important than God.

Golly, without knowledge of good and evil, what is left, Blind Obedience? Did God think that Blind Obedience was going to be the ruling principal in His relationship with His human creation? Was God so bold to think that, if mankind was created in His image[1], mankind would honor Him with blind obedience?

The truth of the matter is that knowledge of good and evil is an essential aspect of life. Without this knowledge what would life be like? That is a good question! My definition of a good question is one that I don't know the answer to or one that I haven't contemplated before. I do not know what life would be like without knowledge of good and evil. The only truth about the knowledge of good and evil that existed at the time of creation would be God's love for what He created. What was the knowledge of good and evil that was imparted to man when the forbidden fruit was eaten? Another good question! Could it concern what can happen when man starts interacting with man? I don't know but it seems plausible. One advisor to this book indicated, "– this isn't a tree of knowledge, but a tree of the knowledge of good and evil. There would be lots we could learn in God's original creation – like chemistry and the orbital period of the moon, etc. But the moral or immoral uses of that knowledge wouldn't be known."[7] Chapters 10 through 14 address "Knowledge" so let's leave how we use knowledge for those chapters.

If God expected mankind to live in His presence with blind obedience, that means that His creation should have nothing but awe for the one who knew so much and would live in comfort obeying God's every command.

You know, I have had many pets in my lifetime. These pets have consisted of several dogs and one cat. The dogs were taught to go to the bathroom outside. They were taught many tricks. They could roll over, reluctantly, on command. They could sit up and beg. They could catch popcorn when it was thrown to them. They could even hold a piece of popcorn on their nose until told to eat it. They could hunt (sometimes). We really taunted them with having them do things that were against their nature. But they did them. Why? Was it blind obedience? Were we "god" to them?

Now the cat, she was something else. No way could she ever be taught to roll over, sit up, catch, or hold something on her nose. She would come when called, but only at her own pace. She could hunt and in fact has brought me many of her treasures, some alive, some dead. Like the dog, she was fed using self feeders that would dispense as needed. As the old story goes, unlike the dog, who thinks its master is "god", the cat thinks that masters behave the way they do because she thinks she is "god".

In both instances, the dogs and the cat were taught to stay off the furniture and not to climb on the counter and generally not to be a pest. As long as we were present, they generally obeyed our teachings. It wasn't blind obedience, however. They knew the consequences if they violated the rule. They would have to be corrected occasionally but generally they would not do the things we didn't want them to do as long as we were there. As soon as we left the house, guess what. Obedience went out the window. The shed hair on the couch or the kitten tracks on the counter always gave them away. What happened to blind obedience when the master was gone?

There goes the truth about blindness. Why can we be blind about obedience when we know darn well that we can see? Perhaps when we cannot see the master, curiosity kicks in. Without the hands on guidance, we become confused. We become impatient. We become worried. What am I going to do? Who is going to take care of me? Who is going to feed me? Am I going to be left out? We start to feel resentment. The master left without us. So, we look for ways to get even or get the master's attention or maybe we can do it all ourselves without the master! The response is, "I know how I'll get even with the master, I'll eat the forbidden fruit"! Wow! Did we ever get even! And just like the dogs and the cat, we paid the price.

The consequences of curiosity can be varied and many. The dogs were put into a cage when the master left. The cat she was locked in a room with food and the sand box. Lucky for us when Eve ate the apple, she did not get locked in a cage or shut in a room. No! For humans, we had to learn to live with one another. God dished out a lot of punishments, but the most severe, in my mind, was this daunting task; we had to learn how to get along!

REFERENCES

1. Genesis 1:1 NLT
2. Genesis 2:5 – Genesis 3:24 NLT
3. Genesis 2:17
4. The Purpose-Driven Life by Rick Warren Copy right 2002 Published by Zondrvan, Grand Rapids, Michigan, 49530
5. Exodus 3: vs. 14
6. **Authors' Note:** God didn't really say that, but that was the author's interpretation of the story and of the consequences.
7. Pastor Rob McPherson, First United Methodist Church, Buchanan, Michigan, cica July, 2006 to the present

DISCUSSION QUESTIONS

1. What would you have done differently if you were God?
2. Do you think the Tree of Knowledge of Good and Evil was a setup?
3. Is conditional love really possible?

THE ORIGINAL SIN

CHAPTER 2

Wouldn't You Rather Have God Take The Consequences?

*My, my, I wonder why
I can't get away without a lie.*

Just think, if Adam and Eve hadn't eaten the fruit from the tree of knowledge of good and evil, we would still be God's children dependent on God for all aspects of our existence. God would be an active integral part of our everyday life, making all of our decisions for us and having a hands on part in our daily affairs. We would be living a care free life, unbound by any responsibility and not subjected to the wills of others who have control issues because they think they know God's will for our lives better than we do.

Bill Huebsch in his book "A New Look At Grace A Spirituality of Wholeness" talks about God's **first exercise of power** (after the creation of the heavens and the earth[1]) was the formation of the human person, the energizing of human beings with life, and imparting the world with spirit[2]. It only stands to reason that He should take the credit for what we are and what we do. After all, we wouldn't be doing what we do if He hadn't created us, Right? As long as God created us, don't you think that God should also take the blame for whatever we do wrong?

Without knowledge of good and evil, we would be like children forever. We would <u>know</u> that our world, our very existence, would be totally dependent on the grace of God instead of thinking that we could exist on our own without that grace.

My daughter sent me an e-mail with the following story which makes my point to a degree:

WHY GOD CREATED CHILDREN (AND IN THE PROCESS GRANDCHILDREN)

Whenever your children are out of control, take comfort that even God's omnipotence did not extend to His own children. After creating the earth and the heavens, God created Adam and Eve. And the first thing He said was;

"Don't"

"Don't what?" Adam replied.

"Don't eat the forbidden fruit." God said.

Forbidden Fruit? We have forbidden fruit? Hey Eve, we have forbidden fruit!"

"No way!" said Eve.

"Yes way!" said Adam.

"Do NOT eat the fruit!" repeated God.

"Why?" said Adam

"Because I am your Father and I said so!" God replied, wondering why He hadn't stopped creation after making the elephants.

A few minutes later, God saw His children having an apple break and He was ticked!

"Didn't I tell you not to eat the fruit?" God asked.

"Uh huh," Adam replied.

"Then why did you?" said the Father.

"I don't know," said Eve.

"She started it!" Adam said.

Having had it with the two of them, God's punishment was that Adam and Eve should have children of their own.

The world seems to be full of blaming others for our actions. Tongue in cheek, we say we did it because of the way we were raised or because we were mistreated when we were growing up. Nothing is our fault. We can't possibly assume responsibility for our actions! Even this action started with Adam. When God asked Adam if he had eaten the forbidden fruit, Adam said "it was that woman you gave me".[3] So Adam blamed God because God gave him "that woman".

If Adam and Eve hadn't learned the truth and gained knowledge about good and evil, we would still be like children. Maybe we wouldn't be doing "things" against God's will, but then, maybe as all children we would. As human beings, we can't help trying to determine our limitations. That is the way God created us. Without knowledge of good and evil, however, we wouldn't know that limitations existed and God would be assuming all of the consequences.

I am certain that we have all heard the excuse that "You owe it to me!" I have heard people tell their employer that the employer owes them a job. I have had employees tell me to be more aware of their need to talk to their friends on the telephone while they are working. Because wearing boots during winter is not fashionable, I have had employees even demand me to shovel a path to their car on a snowy day! A short prayer is in order here, "God please give me patience so that I do not get angry with this nonsense."

Maybe we think that because God is the creator, He owes it to us to give us what ever it is that we want. He owes it to us to give us the best there is. He owes it to us to make our path through life easy.

He owes it to us to give us health and wealth. Maybe He does and maybe He doesn't owe us anything. What we owe Him at least is the willingness to take the first step. What we owe Him is that we are willing to do our part in His creation. God has never asked us to do something that we can't do. All of the resources we need to do a God given task are at our disposal. We owe it to Him to reach out for them. We owe it to Him to take the first step.

God still takes all of the consequences, if we ask Him. Many of us "believe" that God still has an active integral part in our everyday lives while still others "know" that He does. However, we have to remember, "**his second exercise of power** ...was donating this creation back to us"[2], as Bill Huebsch tells us. Basically, God put us in charge. Instead of having God take the blame for everything we do wrong in His creation, we owe Him our appreciation for this second gift by giving God the glory for everything we do right.

The fact is that when Adam and Eve obtained the knowledge of good and evil with their "apple break", the responsibility for human actions shifted. This shift is the crux of many many problems. We have to learn to make good decisions as Pastor David Meister[4] has preached on many occasions. All decisions have consequences. Before the apple break man was without knowledge of good and evil, and God assumed the consequences. Without knowledge of good and evil, we are ignorant. We wouldn't be stupid; we just wouldn't know any better. But God put us in charge of His creation and we can't blame God for our "stupidness", because now we know better. What do we do instead? We avoid the truth. We pretend that the responsibility for our actions belongs to others.

Still, I can't help but wonder what it would be like if God was responsible for everything we do. This "wonder", however, is based on what I know. I know the Ten Commandments. I know, because of the way I was raised, or at least the way I was supposed to be raised, the difference between right and wrong. Without knowledge of good and evil, the requirements of the Ten Commandments would not exist. Without knowledge of good and evil, definition of right and wrong would not exist. Of course, without knowledge of good and evil, there would not be a need for creating a dividing line between right and wrong. Without knowledge of good and evil, the only way would be God's way. All of the consequences would belong to God. God would be directing all of our actions. No boundaries would exist, because there wouldn't be a need for boundaries. The only thing God would want is for us to obey His wishes. Even with knowledge of good and evil, that is all that God asks: obey His Commandments; obey His laws; obey His word. Perhaps I should tone this down a little; after all, God did give us free will. Maybe we should have the desire to obey!

Unlike our constitution, the word of God cannot be amended. No process exists to change Gods word. His command is final. His word is perfect and requires no amendment. God takes an active part in our lives whether you believe it or not. He doesn't just wind us up like a watch and leave us to do what we are going to do. It doesn't make any difference whether we have knowledge of good and evil or not. God's way is the only way. It is not his fault if we choose to go against His will. The consequences are both ours and His. If we ask, He will take the responsibility. But, if we ask, expiation demands that we do it His way because we want to. God sends nothing but silence as He honors us with the freedom to choose whether or not we want a relationship with Him, or as Max Lucado says "choose where to spend eternity"[5]. Fortunately, as children we learned manners and we learned not to interrupt. As adults, some of us have responded by backing off so far that we find it difficult to interact with people, while others have learned to interact vociferously, and still others have learned to interact by listening and learning. We may still think that we are the center of the universe, but our universe has changed. We have redefined our universe so that we can be the center. All of us like to be in control of our universe. If we find that we are not in control, we redefine our universe so that we can be in control. The nature of the control may be a demanding imposition on others or it may be a placid introverted "back offish" response. Most of us are somewhere in between. The truth of the matter is that God is in control.

In the first place, maybe we shouldn't be doing things that requires God to take the consequences. Without knowledge of good and evil, how do we know what not to do? Did God ever intend for His creation to NOT suffer the consequences? Even existing in bliss has its consequences. Let's face it, life without consequences is impossible even if God takes the consequences. The fact remains, we do have "the benefit" of Eve eating of the fruit from the tree of knowledge of good and evil and we are eternally paying the consequences. Imagining what life would be like without consequences is impossible. But yes, we can consider doing things that require God to take the consequences. In fact, I believe that we would all benefit from letting God have all of the glory from our actions. If we were to work toward the goal of letting our actions generate a consequence that is glorifying to God, I think that we would have fulfilled the original intention of allowing humankind to think for themselves. I can imagine the smile on God's face now.

Are we smart enough to know the consequences now that we have knowledge of good and evil? Sometimes I think that we are too smart and we believe that we don't have to think about the consequences. The pleasure of the moment seems to be the guiding light rather than how the pleasure will affect the welfare of self and others. Consequences be damned! Hooray for me and to hell with everybody else. My Dad used to lecture me about that attitude when I was growing up. I didn't pay much attention to the lecture because he also had the attitude that I should do as he said and not as he did! On the other hand, the lectures about only thinking of myself instead of the consequences of my actions have helped me to at least consider the consequences. But I think the biggest problem is to be able to consider "all" of the consequences. I have never learned to be able to think beyond what I can see in the immediate future and beyond those who are involved at the moment. I don't know about you but, I have had events where I have done things that I have regretted because I didn't think about the consequences down the road nor did I think about how what I did would impact people that were not involved only to find out later that I was wrong.

Did God ever intend to allow His human creation to exist without consequences? Did He think that we would be able to function in the innocence of existence without knowledge of good and evil? I am certain that you would agree with me that the guilty feeling that goes along with the consequences of bad decisions would be a welcomed loss in our emotional world. (That is not about to happen!) But, if we didn't know about good and evil, would there be consequences? Let's see! A world without consequences or a world with consequences, which would I choose?

What would a world without consequences be like? First of all, I think that we would have to reintroduce that notion of bovine passivity. We would go through life innocently attending to our business without any relationship to acts that were neither good nor evil. There would be no distinction between good or bad acts and therefore no consequences. Would all of our acts be "good"? I don't think so, but it wouldn't be bad either! Isn't it interesting how we judge our actions? Without knowledge of good and evil, can we assume that all would be good? Our actions would be without consequences because nothing would exist that would allow us to judge those actions. It's our knowledge of "good" and "evil" that introduces one of the most condemning consequences, guilt. What's more, not all "good" is judged the same by all people as "good" and not all "evil" is judged by all people as "evil".

Lord have mercy! Please make this "good' and "evil" thing "black" and "white" so we can have the same understanding and eliminate the judging! AMEN!

A deist believes in a remote God that created earth and has no active part in the on going affairs of earth. A theist believes God continues to be an active part in all things in his creation. ALL THINGS! I had a boss who once drew a picture of a "thing" on one of my reports when I used that word. In this instance, however, "all things" means "all things". There isn't anything that you can imagine that is not included!

In all things God works for good. And we know that God causes everything to work together for the good of those who love God and are called according to his purpose for them[6]. In all things God works in me for good. So, yes! God knows the consequences! And yes, God intended for all of our actions to be good. How do I know this? Because we are God's creation and our actions are for His glory. If we can pull ourselves away from judgmental appreciation of other's actions and think about "all things" being for the glory of God, knowledge of "evil" can be less harsh.

In an old radio show, "Life of Riley"[7], after he messed up a situation, Riley apologized to his wife, Peg, and told her that he didn't have a mind of his own so he used everybody else's and it got him into trouble. We have a tendency to do the same thing when we are in trouble. When we don't have a mind of our own; we use somebody else's. Sometimes we are smart enough to use God's mind, or at least His guidance. If we go back to His creation and identify the talents that He has given us, we can determine the route to take to get out of trouble, or to stay out of trouble, or to avoid trouble in the first place.

We all think that what we know is what is best for everybody else. We use our knowledge and what we have learned to judge what is best for everybody around us. The knowledge that each of us has is the center of our individual universes. What is good enough for us is good enough for everybody else. Original sin is like that. We forget that the universe is full of knowledge that we don't know. We forget that knowledge is all around us. We forget that the vastness of creation is beyond our comprehension. We forget that the center of the universe is the Creator. We forget that we are the created and not the creator. Another short prayer is in order: "God forgive us and lead us into the kingdom of right relationships!"

REFERENCES

1. Genesis 2:4
2. Bill Huebsch "A New Look At Grace A Spirituality of Wholeness" p74, Twenty-third Publications A Division of Bayard, Mystic, CT 06355
3. Genesis 3:12
4. David Meister was pastor of the First United Methodist Church of Buchanan, Michigan, from 2003 to 2006.
5. From "He Chose the Nails" by Max Lucado
6. Romans 8, v28
7. "Life of Riley" Broadcast, May 13, 1945

DISCUSSION QUESTIONS

1. Do consequences really work?
2. Would you rather have GOD, or someone else, making all your decisions, or do you enjoy having free will?
3. Does free will make you responsible for your actions, and therefore, the accompanying consequences?

THE SNAKE

CHAPTER 3

How Did The Snake Get So Smart?

No matter how we wiggle and squirm,
Evil amongst us goads us to learn!

God's creation included many "creatures". There was a purpose for them all. God knows the purpose, but we have to learn them because we are not God. What else was in the Garden? Man was put in the garden to till it and keep it[1]. So, we can imagine that man would be exploring God's creation in order to learn more about his responsibility.

Was man, or in this instance woman, just wandering around looking to see what was available and to determine what else needed tilling and to be kept? Maybe she was looking to see what she could eat of freely. Low and behold, she encountered the forbidden tree, the tree of the knowledge of good and evil. At that time there just happened to be a snake in the tree. The snake creature was more subtle than any other wild creature that God had made[2]. The snake was part of God's original creation, more subtle than all of the rest. Did man know that? I doubt it. But, here is woman in her most curious form trying to learn all that there is to learn about God's creation and up pops the snake with all of its subtlety.

Most of us have at least some difficulty accepting snakes as creatures that God has made for us to care for or "keep" as it says in Genesis[2]. I have handled a few harmless garter snakes, but I have not really accepted them as a creature that I would go out of the way to help or to "keep". I have a very dear friend who is extremely fearful of snakes. This friend is so spooked at the mere thought of snakes that she can't even say the word "snake". Instead, she, when she has to include them in a conversation, will referee to them as "kitties". I don't know what she has against cats, but it is sort of a joke among this circle of friends that she calls snakes kitties.

So, I don't know what the snake was hoping to accomplish with its first encounter with man in the Garden of Eden, but, I think it got more than it bargained for. Just look at the consequences to the snake[3]; "The Lord said to the serpent, "Because you have done this, cursed are you above all cattle, and above all wild animals; upon your belly you shall go, and dust you shall eat all the days of your life."

I don't know what the snake was doing before it chose to confront the woman, but what ever it was, I am sure it wasn't expecting this vehement reaction from its creator. I think we all are that way. We go about enjoying creation and worshipping God in the way that we think God wants and all of a sudden, we are confronted with a "What the hell were you thinking" response from God. But just like the snake, we are not innocent and our subtlety is very transparent. I am certain that the snake knew exactly what it was doing. I also submit that we know exactly what we are doing. TESTING!!! Where are the fence lines? How far can we go before we get a reaction? What can we get away with before someone says that we have gone too far? Often times, the response comes from a direction that we were not expecting. Just like the snake.

The snake was expecting something different than it received. Could it be that the snake was measuring a response from the woman that would be one of gratitude versus a response from God that would be one of retribution? The gratitude would be for learning the difference between good and evil and for all of the "knowledge". The retribution would be from God for enticing this woman creature. Instead, the snake received something entirely different, condemnation. Perhaps, the snake was looking to be included in the windfall of wisdom so that it could exploit its subtle nature even further. Then, just like us humans, up pops the Creator reminding us it isn't about us. The response was way beyond what the snake expected. Creation is for God! The Garden was created for God; the snake was created for God; man was created for God; and woman was created for God (and for man as a "helper"[4], I just had to throw in that part).

Before man was created, the snake was the only subtle creature in the garden! It probably got away with using its subtle nature with other creatures in the garden because the subtleness was of no consequence. The intelligence of the snake was the result of being on its own in the middle of creation without the need to be responsible for its actions. It was created to be a snake and that is what it did. Each day it became a little smarter as it learned how to exploit its God given talents to survive.

Just like us, we can "get away with" exploiting our nature, if it is of no consequence. That is to say, the features of our nature can be used to improve our nature for the glory of God. But, the moment we use these features to better ourselves without God, it becomes offensive and retribution will surely occur somehow. In this instance, the snake encountered the subtleness of man or more specifically, of woman and the shit hit the fan. It got God's attention big time.

Maybe God should have been giving His attention to issues in the garden in the first place. Where was God when the snake was tempting Eve? Was God just waiting for his subtle creatures to encounter each other? Was He testing His creation to determine how far they could be trusted? I think we already went over that in Chapter 1.

But still, there are times when we wonder; "Where is God's attention when we really need it?" How can He let me fall victim to such an obvious plot. After all, Eve could not have been tempted if God had said the entire garden is yours to till and keep. But he didn't. He left that one silly tree as a no-no just waiting for a subtle creature to come along and tempt another subtle creature.

Where was God? Why did He think just saying "no" was enough? You have to consider that at this point in creation, in addition to being subtle, man was very naive. He didn't know any better. He didn't know any worse either. He didn't have any knowledge of good and evil. Man was left with his only purpose to till and keep. Being tempted was bound to happen. After all, the tree was there and so was the snake. The snake had been there for a while and had no competition for its subtleness. If God wanted us to remain naïve, shouldn't He have been there to help man with this temptation conundrum. Shouldn't God have been there to protect His creation as it was originally intended before the temptation occurred instead of after?

I have news for you, He was there! He is always there! He knows that we cannot do it alone. He is not waiting for us to prove how smart we are or how independent we are, he is waiting for us to acknowledge that we need his help. The snake was the first lesson to prove to us that as independent as we think we are, God knows we will find out that we cannot do it without acknowledging that God is the creator and we cannot do it without Him. He is there to help

I think that we all tend to wait just to see what happens when we probably should be stepping in and doing something to protect God's creation. What are we waiting for? A snake? Are we expecting God to push us into action? Do we have to encounter a snake in order to recognize God's will? Even in the Garden of Eden, man knew it was wrong, **period**. God doesn't need to be there to hold our hand to show us what is wrong. Although, we would definitely like the support sometimes, He doesn't need to be there even though He is.

What makes us think that we can go about our existence without acknowledging that God had anything to do with it? We have to conscientiously acknowledge that He is there and that the support is there. We have to take that first step. He has created us with some common sense and we are expected to use it. We cannot feign ignorance, and we cannot go through life blaming the snake. He has already told us what is expected. So why do we keep trying to find out where the boundaries are? Testing, we are always testing! The snake knew where the boundaries were by his very subtle nature. The snake had already experienced living in creation, but had nothing to challenge its subtle nature. Then God created man!

As a consequence of its actions, the snake was made to go on his belly[5]. So, how did the snake get around before it tempted Eve? Perhaps, it still slithered but maybe it had its head a little higher before the temptation affair. After the temptation, God had the snake eating dust all the days of its life[5]. When we find out that we have crossed the boundary into the realm of disappointment, don't all of us conscientious people hang our head in shame? Don't we eat a little humble pie (dirt)? We willingly acknowledge that we should have known better. So, why did we do these things any way? Perhaps like the snake, we weren't smart enough to think of all of the consequences. We were expecting a reaction that was meant to be positive, at least as far as we were thinking for ourselves. We crawl around in our own little world failing to accept that we are part of a bigger creation and that we can't do it without God.

Our actions may be meant to better our circumstances, but that is the problem. We have considered them as our circumstances when in fact our intentions involve much more than our little part of creation. How can we learn to hold our head up and look around to be certain that our actions create a positive effect for all of creation and not just the little part that we seemed to think represents the most important part of God's creation?

The snake in the garden tempting Eve to eat the fruit of the tree of the knowledge of good and evil raises another interesting question. Did the snake already know about good and evil? This question paints an entirely different picture. If the snake didn't know the difference, that is one thing. Then the snake was only trying to undermine God's authority without knowing the consequences and the snake got what it deserved. On the other hand, if the snake knew the difference between good and evil and also knew that Eve didn't have that knowledge, the snake was really going the distance to gather an accomplice on its evil journey.

Adam and Eve deserve a tremendous pat on the back for recognizing that they crossed a forbidden boundary and for looking to God for help to get back into His good graces. They ultimately did exactly as we should all do, acknowledge to God that we were wrong and thank God for being part of His creation.

"Good and evil" did not have its beginning with the first bite of the forbidden fruit! <u>Knowledge</u> of "good and evil" had its beginning in mankind when Eve took that bit. We know that God created "Good". Just look at the first creation story[6]. The "evil" part wasn't recognized until humans went against God's goodness for their own desires. The snake probably already knew about "good and evil". After all, the snake was created with a subtle nature. So how did the snake get so smart? I think we can believe that the subtle nature of the snake was the consequence of knowing about good and evil in the first place and he couldn't wait to have an accomplice.

REFERENCES

1. Genesis 2:15
2. Genesis 3:1
3. Genesis 3: 14
4. Genesis 2: 18
5. Genesis 3: 14
6. Genesis 1:1 – Genesis 2:4

DISCUSSSION QUESTIONS

1. How do you fend off temptations?
2. Was the snake actually the first appearance of the devil?
3. Why is it so easy to be evil and so difficult to be good?

THE SNAKE

CHAPTER 4

What Was in It for the Snake?

*Troubles begin with thoughts for me
When they really should be thoughts for Thee!*

So what was the snake up to? This cunning subtle creature of God had something devious on its mind. You can be certain of that. As much as we would like to believe that God put the snake on earth so that we could blame it for our deviation from the perfect relationship that God wanted, such is not the case. Isn't that just like us? We think the whole crux of this story is about us! Wrong!

That snake was looking for something. It was expecting to gain some advantage. No doubt about it, the snake had an ulterior motive. All of our actions, in my opinion, have ulterior motives and the snake was no exception. As subtle as we may think we are, we are always looking for a leg up to something. We are trying to prove a point; or we are trying to impress someone; or we are trying to show how smart we are; or we are trying to corner the market on sympathy; or we are trying to be worthy of some ones love; or we are trying to prove that God is on our side and likes us better. Whatever the issue, seldom do we think it is for God's glory first. We don't think about becoming less so that God can become more. Oh, I am not trying to say that we don't think of God, but, often times, we don't think of God soon enough. Neither did the snake! He had an ulterior motive.

Having found myself on many occasions trying to maneuver others to my advantage, it is easy for me to considering the subtle nature of "Snake". I don't believe its motivation was any different than yours or mine given the right situations. Just like us it was calculating some kind of gain. Snake undoubtedly had contemplated what it could gain and was going to do whatever it could to accomplish the task. Snake wasn't doing this deed to simply make itself look better in the mirror; it was doing this deed to have an image that impressed someone or something. It calculated that, if it succeeded, Snake was going to look better than the foolish humans that God had created. It had calculated that the outcome would provide a new situation that would be to its benefit and advantage. Snake knew that the advantage would be better than any loss it could possibly imagine. Little did it know? Just like us, Snake didn't look far enough.

This calculating, devious, cunning, subtle creature was looking to exploit the humans for its own purpose. Snake had already determined that it was going to use temptation to accomplish the task designed to achieve a gain at the expense of the humans. Did Snake have anything else on its mind? Was it considering failure with its plan? Did Snake adequately think through all of the consequences or did it only see that sparkling advantage that presented itself in Snake's imagination? What possible advantage did Snake visualize? In its mind, Snake probably had nothing to loose. On the other hand, creation was so new that it didn't have anything to gauge against potential loss. This first encounter with humans was different than the encounters with all of the rest of creation. Its subtle nature found a new challenge to exploit. Hmmm! For some reason, this sound familiar.

The snake thought that achieving whatever gains it visualized were worth the risks, at least as far as the snake could visualize the risks. What could the snake possibly visualize it could loose? Already a low life, Snake really didn't have anything to loose, did it? Was it so desperate that it was willing to risk what little it had to gain whatever advantage it visualized? I don't think so. For that, I guess, we can thank the snake. It showed us that there is always something to loose, even when you are the low life of creation. But have we learned? Do we still try to spend our talents on devious advantages?

What does it take for us to be willing to risk all that we have? Have we ever been desperate enough to risk everything we have? I think that we always try to hold something back and so did the snake.

Was the snake jealous of man? Maybe if Snake could prove man was less trustworthy than it was, God would put it in charge of the Garden! After all, being in charge of the Garden would be an awesome powerful opportunity and the snake with its subtle nature knew it. Power! What a driving force. Control! What glorious things can be attained if we only had control? Somehow, Snake knew the nature of God, or at least it thought it did, and believed that if it gained some advantage over God's chosen creatures, it would become the "God" creature. All Snake had to do was get recognized, get God's attention and prove that it was smarter than man. Poor man! Man didn't even know he was being used. He didn't have a chance against this first encounter with another subtle creature. In fact, man didn't even know he could be subtle until he learned it from the snake. Look what has happened. The snake has added to our repertoire and turned us into a skeptical creature as well, but I don't believe that was its intent. Isn't that just like us? We think it is all about us!

Snake wasn't thinking about us and it wasn't thinking about God either. We can tell it wasn't thinking about God. Otherwise, it would not have ended up being the eternal low life that it is. I can "garendamntee" you that Snake did not get what it was expecting. No way in hell did it get what it wanted. (Well, maybe in hell it got what it wanted.) The consequence of its actions was more than what Snake wanted or expected.

So what did Snake want? Since it didn't get what it wanted, I am not certain that we know. However, with a little imagination, we can guess. Snake was looking to be held in high esteem somehow. How can we guess that? It's easy. Snake, we are told, Genesis 3:1, had a subtle nature. It was looking for something that it hoped would be beyond the perceptive ability of most on-lookers. Sort of like "you can fool some of the people all of the time and you can fool all of the people some of the time, but you can't fool all of the people all of the time." Snake thought it had more power than God and was using its God given talent (subtle nature) to show how it could independently control his world. Yet here we are still trying to be like Snake! In some ways, it seems that Snake did get what it wanted, since later it is called the "god of this world[1]" and even in the temptations of Christ[2] seems to have legitimate authority over the kingdoms of the earth.

The world is full of control freaks. We all do it. Some of us try so hard for control that the rest of the world is suffocated with the domineering attitude that we present. Somebody has to be in control, but who should it be? Either it is going to be us or we pass up the opportunity because the person who gets pissed off the most will take it out on us if he doesn't get the job. Snake was trying to find out if it had enough power to take control. It couldn't wait to be given control because it knew that its subtle nature was not enough. Power and glory belong to God!

Can you imagine thinking that you can tempt God into giving up control? Snake did, and so do a lot of us! Why else would Snake be tempting man with an apple. Snake's subtle nature almost worked. It worked enough to get Eve to take a bite and enough to get Adam to do the same. But God had had enough! He reacted with a response that even subtle Snake was not expecting. Tempt God indeed! God is not about to relinquish control. This is His creation and no one or no thing is about to gain some advantage over it. That is impossible. God may let us go about our tasks thinking, like Snake, that we can use our talents to our advantage, but about the time that we think we have managed to out fox the Creator, his creating abilities respond with a humbling experience and we eat dust.

No matter what Snake wanted, no matter what Snake was hoping to achieve, one thing is certain, snakes do not rule. This snake did prove one thing; God is in control. Snake can tempt all it wants, God is in control. Control takes more than a subtle nature or a bad disposition. The subtle part of God's creation that exists in us where we think we can get away with something that will give us an advantage or at least what we think will be an advantage is not subtle to God. It is an insult! In the case of Snake, and man, in the Garden of Eden, what took place with that stupid apple pissed God off. Nobody got what they wanted. Snake didn't get control and man did not become as smart as God. However, both got more than they bargained for.

REFERENCES

1. 2 Corinthians 4;4
2. Mathew 4:1-11

DISCUSSSION QUESTIONS

1. Have you ever used your position to deceive someone?
2. So, does deception make you feel in charge, or guilty?
3. Is GOD your first resort or your last resort?

THE SNAKE

CHAPTER 5

What Good Is Deception Without Someone To Deceive?

Who are we trying to fool?
God knows what we can rule.

So Snake had an ulterior motive! Its motive was worth nothing without having a receptor for its devices. Snake saw a patsy and lay in wait for her to appear. Snake didn't know how far it could go, but once the deception process started, it was easy to take the process to an end that even Snake didn't expect. I can't help but think that Snake was testing the vulnerability of the human creature and we took the bait hook, line, and sinker. We bit with a desire reserved for only someone wanting to learn as much as possible in as quickly as possible.

Our receptors are always open looking for an opportunity to gain that advantage. So why was Eve looking for this opportunity? Maybe she wasn't. Maybe she was a victim of circumstances. Ya right! Just like Snake was a victim of opportunity! Eve was no different than the snake. She was doing the same thing, thinking that she could be as knowledgeable as God. Eve was about to learn that there was more to God than knowledge of good and evil. In fact she was about to learn that knowledge of good and evil comes with a price tag!

Did God create her ready to be deceived or was this God's gift of free will? For a fact, she was not a puppet! All of us fall into this state to one degree or another. We all have myopic powers to only think about what has been laid out for ourselves. This channel vision is not capable of the panoramic view needed to see all of the peripheral consequences. We set ourselves up to be victims of deception. We think that "if only" we had this one piece, the rest of the picture would come into view and we would be able to complete the puzzle in no time at all.

Let's get back to Snake. As I think about this, the movie series Star Wars with Darth Vader and the Jedis[4] come to mind. Good v. evil! Darth Vader (Snake) switching to the "Dark Side" with the "self first" drive for the sole purpose of controlling all mankind. At the same time, the Jedis were working against the dark side for the goodness of all mankind. Living a life that puts self first needs someone else to exploit! Snake was trying to exploit this "self first" nature for its own purpose and so was this human creature. The dark side was there, so where were the Jedis?

With Darth Vader in mind, the dark side of our nature comes into view. "Snakes" live on the dark side and have accepted that view as the driving force in their lives. Mankind can be a victim of this dark side in two ways. First, "snakes" count on the naiveté that is associated with human's thinking their independence is strong enough to resist the apples that are extended. Secondly, man can be convinced that Snake is right and accept its offer of the "dark side life". Snake can exploit the "goodness" of man. We have already explored the first way in Chapter 4. But what is it about this more sinister side that drives humans to accept the deception that evil has more advantages than good? More importantly, what is it about thinking that being "good" allows us to even have a notion that we can toy with evil and get away with it?

If Snake had not already "eaten the apple" and chosen evil, it would not have been tempting Eve. Snake had accepted the evil side and was letting that evil drive its life. The only way Snake could exist was to live off of the goodness in the world. And, in this instance it wasn't only goodness, it was the absence of knowledge of good and evil that Snake was exploiting. This absence of knowledge is a poor crutch and we have already dealt with this aspect to a degree. We will discuss knowledge further in Chapters 10 – 14. For now, we have to accept that Snake knew what it was doing and was counting on the notion that humans, like itself, had an interest in learning how to become the go to person when God wasn't around.

That is the issue isn't it? We think that we can go behind God's back. We think that God isn't "watching". Technically, Genesis teaches us that we can hide[1]. When we do, we set ourselves up to be deceived because we believe that we have been left behind. In reality, we haven't been left behind. We are the ones that have left God behind. We have not allowed God to be the recipient of the glory of our actions. We want the glory, and because we want the glory, we are vulnerable to the forces of the dark side.

I can remember an occasion when I was about 11 or 12 and was dependent on my parents for everything, or so I thought. On this particular occasion, I had come home from school and no one was home. I was left behind. Where had my parents gone without me? Where was my brother? He was younger than me by about two years. Had my parents taken him some where without me? Why didn't they take me? There was no note explaining where they were or how long they would be gone. I was very frustrated and angry that they would even consider going somewhere without me and not even tell me or consult with me or include me. I was so angry in fact that I broke a window in the garage door for no reason except that I was angry.

When my parents returned home, I lied about the window and told them that a burglar had tried to gain entrance to the house. They sure believed that story alright. Ya, right on this one too! I got a "whoopin" for breaking the window and had to pay for replacing it out of my meager allowance. I don't remember for sure, but I would bet that my father even made me do the work replacing the window just to show me that I couldn't just buy my way out of the lie.

It was amazing what little it took for me to believe that I had been abandoned! Not only that, but my mind had conjured up the idea that I had been abandoned in favor of someone else. In reality the whole situation was blown so far out of proportion that the actual reality of the occasion has become obscure and escapes me. I think that my parents had simply gone grocery shopping and had been delayed and lost track of time. They were home within fifteen minutes after I got home and my brother walked home from school a short time after I got home.

During the short interval, however, I was vulnerable to deception. Did you notice how much the situation was about me? Why was this happening to ME? We can become so susceptible to deception that we can deceive ourselves. I came home expecting to find my parents there waiting for me. I was expecting to be included in whatever was going to happen once I got home. This single event so impacted me that while our children were growing up, leaving notes on our whereabouts was an integral part of our lives. If we weren't there in person, a note saying where we were and when to expect us was left. Even today I leave notes for my wife, even if she knows where I am. I sign them all JBILY (Just Because I Love You).

Having lost track of my parents, I had lost faith in my parent's ability to take care of me. For a 12 year old, this was devastating and I became vulnerable to deception. The deception was that anger would bring them back. I became susceptible to the dark side and I lied thinking I could cover up my lack of faith. I didn't want my parents to think I had lost faith in them and become angry because they weren't where I thought they should be. I didn't want them to think I wasn't capable of existing on my own for a short time. To this day they don't really know why I did what I did. Neither do I. What good could I think would come from breaking that damn window? Did I think that action would cause them to pay more attention to me? Maybe they would think twice the next time they would leave me behind and take my brother instead of me. That would teach them not be at home when I thought they should be! I am positive they got that message. Isn't that something! Our minds can really exaggerate the significance of a situation. We can blow the situations way out of proportion.

The same thing can happen when we loose track of God. We become vulnerable to deception. In fact, we can become so lost when we loose track of God, we think the only way is our way. At those times, we are most vulnerable to deception from the full time snakes. They are looking for souls to steal and our souls are bared most when we loose track of God. Our faith is at its lowest ebb when we loose track of God. What good is faith if we don't use it? Faith believes that something doesn't require proof to exist. Faith believes that God is the creator and doesn't require proof.

Why do we believe that God isn't looking? Have we deceived ourselves into thinking that God isn't there when we want to experience the dark side of his creation? God trusts that our belief in Him as the creator will be all that we need to overcome the temptations to live without Him. Why is it so hard to trust God in return for being there when we need Him?

I have a friend who tells about calling the manufacturer of his fishing pole for a replacement when he broke the tip of his rod. The manufacturer was willing to send him the replacement free of charge. All my friend had to do was give the manufacturer his credit card number to pay $6.00 for the shipping. My friend was not willing to trust the manufacturer with his credit card information. The manufacturer said that was OK. He asked my friend to simply send him a check for the shipping cost once my friend received the pole tip. Not only did my friend get the tip, the manufacturer sent him two of them and trusted him to send the required check. What good is faith if you don't use it?

When we think that God has abandoned us, maybe we need to look somewhere else. If we can't seem to find God maybe we are looking in the wrong places. God is there and it is impossible to go behind His back. Trying to get God's attention because we think He has abandoned us is only an excuse for our desire to experience the dark side. In the case with Eve, Snake saw an opportunity to gain a convert. It knew that Eve was vulnerable to deception. She was wandering around in the garden looking for an opportunity to experience something without God. She thought that God wasn't looking. Snake saw its chance. "Hey, Eve, try this apple. It won't kill you like God said. Look at me. I'm not dead!" Come on Eve, what secrets did you think the snake had that God didn't have? Where did your faith go? Did you think that God had left you behind? Did you think that God was holding out on you? Did you think your short span of life needed more excitement? Whatever you thought, Eve, Snake saw you coming. It knew you were ripe for deception, a little naïve maybe, living in the Garden, but ripe just the same. Was this part of God's plan from the beginning?

We know that God has not abandoned us. We know that God has not taken someone else in our place. We know that God has not left us behind. We know that God has not left us vulnerable to deception. Our vulnerability is only in our mind. Our acceptance of God requires faith and what good is faith if you don't use it. Existing without faith is no excuse for blaming God if we get tempted by a snake. And it is certainly no excuse if we accept the temptation as being better than what God has to offer. Who has abandoned whom? Even Jesus asked on the night he was betrayed "God why have you abandoned me?[2]" when he knew better. Jesus simply didn't want to go through with the act that he knew was coming. Actually, Jesus was looking in the right place and his faith had never waivered[3]! Indeed, what good is faith if you don't use it!

Taking an apple may get God's attention but the attention God gives you may not be what you were looking for. Taking an apple from a snake certainly got God's attention for Adam and Eve. Believing that God will be there when we need Him got us a savior. We will always be vulnerable to snakes because we are vulnerable to deception. The free will that we received will always be challenged. The faith that we have in the creator will always be the defense against the dark side. Deception is only in our minds because we let it be there. We think that we can go behind God's back and experience the dark side without getting hooked. In fact, we are so bold that we think that we can deceive God. Like our parents have told us, we have another "think" coming.

REFERENCES

1. Genesis 3:10
2. Mathew 27:46
3. Psalm 22
4. **Star Wars** is an American epic space opera franchise conceived by George Lucas. The first film in the franchise was originally released on May 25, 1977, by 20th Century Fox

DISCUSSION QUESTIONS

1. Have you ever been to the "Dark Side"?
2. Why are we sometimes so easily deceived?
3. So, you have been to the "Dark Side", and you have been deceived. Did you reach out to GOD and ask for his guidance?

THE SNAKE

CHAPTER 6

Vertebrate Or Invertebrate?
Are You Standing Or Slithering?

Thinking for ourselves alone
Requires us to have a "backbone".

"Snakes" as created in Genesis 2 and 3 and persons that follow their example exist on deception, conniving, exploitation and otherwise taking advantage of the goodness in this world. They know their way around honesty. In fact, their very existence is dependent on people who are less than honest with themselves. So then, how many snakes does it take to make a snake pit? For sure, at least two! But, who is taking advantage of whom? While one snake may have its sights set on using a person to its advantage, the other snake is thinking that it is going to get something for nothing or close to it; otherwise, no deal would be struck.

The "true snakes" in this world absolutely know that the crux of their existence is temptation. They absolutely know that everyone has a weak spot they can use to their advantage. However, they also know that reaching the weak spot is easier with some people than others. Obviously, Snake prefers easier picking of the low hanging fruit. But if it has to, it will climb a tree.

Just think of what others can find to use in our lives. My, oh my! The world is full of opportunities to become better persons in our own minds. The perspective we use to build our own image is more than the visage we see in the mirror. How many "things" can we live without? Or better yet how many "things" can we not live without?

It is those "things" we want to live with that cause us to become victims of temptation. Jesus in the wilderness, after his baptism, was tempted with food, testing God, and power[1]. If only we could have that kind of backbone to stand up to the snakes in this world.

So, ok, we are not as disciplined as Jesus! Tell us something new! But still, until we understand what can be used to temp us, we are vulnerable to the snakes. Even then, our perspective can be clouded with the "apples" that the snake some how can find to dangle in front of us. Snakes are dedicated to existing just like the rest of us. However, different from most of us, snakes have made a total commitment to a life that is parasitic.

Although "snakes" may be parasites, they are not worried about choking the life out of the host. They know that as long as people exist, there will be those who want to be a snake even if it is just for an instant or two. There will always be some one who wants to entice temptation. Why? Because we all think we are strong enough and smart enough to get away with it and not get caught. Wrong! We have deluded ourselves into thinking that accepting a temptation only matters to us and that no one else is watching; and that no one else will suffer the consequences; and that no one else will think it is important to them. We can't tempt temptation for even a minute without becoming a snake ourselves.

From its first experience with Eve, Snake knew that it could be the tempter. But what else did it gain from this first experience? It gained the knowledge that a world of wannabes was available. It gained the knowledge that it could always find a patsy. It gained the knowledge that it didn't need any worldly possessions of its own to be a tempter. It found out that it could pretend to have what others wanted and get away with it. Sort of like Bernard Madolff and his Ponzi schemes[2]. Ultimately, it gained "the privilege" of being a snake for the rest of its life. Snake took its punishment and slithered off to get ready for the next opportunity. It knew that it wouldn't take long for it to arrive.

What did Eve gain? She got her patties spanked, didn't she? When you think about the "incident" from this perspective, it becomes clear that if Eve had wanted to become a snake at that point she certainly could have. She could have joined forces with Snake and gone permanently to the snake pit right along side Snake. The choices we make when we are caught red handed speak volumes about the kind of person we have the potential to be. Here she was in the middle of utopia and didn't know how good she had it. Here she was trying to become as smart as God and didn't know that she was as smart as she needed to be. Here she was taking a bite of the forbidden fruit and she knew better. What's more, here she was dragging someone else into the snake pit with her. Boy, was that easy or what? What was Adam thinking anyway? For that matter where was Adam all this time? But that is someone else's story[12].

Eve had nothing to gage the consequence of her actions against. No experience existed that would permit her to compare results. As we all know, she was about to experience the wrath of God. Still, what did she gain? She managed somehow to keep from becoming a permanent snake, but that is not much of a gain. She managed to stir up the unwanted attention of God, but I don't believe she gained anything from that except to learn what a "no no" will gain her. She managed to get Adam in trouble too, but that was no gain for her except it may have taken a little of the wrath of God off of her. (Some say that Adam got himself into trouble. After all he was an adult and was lead astray with his own desires.) Most of all, she managed to get into trouble with God, but that was no gain either. What did she gain?

Considering the consequences, Eve gained considerably, although what she gained was not what she was expecting. She was expecting to gain something she didn't have; otherwise she wouldn't have taken the chance. She was tempted to do more than simply defy God. I am certain that she didn't know what to expect from God but whatever her mind could conger up, to her it was worth the risk. Snake knew the answer; she wanted to be like God[3], and to be wise[4]. That did it! Snake had it first victim! The desire to be something or someone without going through the proper channels caused her to be tempted; taking a short cut. Snake connived and Eve bought it. She got wiser alright, but she didn't get wiser about the Godly things and she definitely found out there was more to being like God than being created in His image.

When Eve, for the first time, gained the pain of experiencing the knowledge that she had gone against the will of God, also gained a conscience that would not allow her to go another step without feeling guilty about what she had done. She felt so guilty that she sought company so she wouldn't have to handle the pain alone. She became a snake for another instant when Adam came along. Now both of them gained the same thing. The sinking feeling in the pit of their stomachs didn't get any better. Sharing that sensation does not make it less. As a matter of fact it makes it worse. Just look at what they did. They hid[5]! They hid from God and they hid from each other. They tried to cover it up, but the fig leaf[6] wasn't sufficient. They got caught anyway.

What made Eve decide not to become a full time snake? I'll bet you know! I'll bet that you can feel that same empty sensation in the pit of your stomach right now just thinking about being caught red handed accepting a temptation. What brought them back to reality was the realization that they had violated a trust. At that point, they had a choice. A choice! They could be like Snake and slither away or they could stand up for themselves and try to get back into the good graces of God.

That sinking feeling they experienced when they were caught red handed was new for them and they didn't like it. The numbing sensations that went along with this new experience were not comfortable. They obviously preferred the loving relationship they had with God before they took the apple and ate it. That God loving relationship was an experience they could understand and an experience that felt "right".

The punishment God metered out was harsh; the pain of child birth and the desire for men[7]. (I can hear Snakes conniving now!) Some would argue that the "desire for men" was anything but harsh. Based on my experience, the harshest punishment for both Eve and Adam most likely was the punishment for Eve, "but man will rule over her"[7], although they didn't know it yet. Adam was punished with hard work to survive[8] and was forced from the Garden of Eden[9].

Yet, they accepted their punishment. They accepted God's way despite the punishment. They didn't slither away. They stood up and took their licks. It was their choice. They could have chosen to continue along the path that departed from God's way but they didn't. They didn't have a choice about the punishment but they did have a choice as to their relationship with God. They chose to try to stay on God's good side. They chose to accept responsibility for their actions. They didn't say it was Snake's fault. They didn't try to blame God for putting the tree there in the first place. Although they tried to blame each other (because there were two of them), they didn't have anyone to blame except themselves.

In this day and age, when we accept the temptations "the snakes" offer and we get caught, like Adam[10], we blame anyone and anything we can. We blame our parents, or the nuns, or the school, or the movies we see, or the songs we hear, or the other guy. On and on, we have a plethora of excuses available to us. What softies we are. Even though Adam blamed God10, Adam and Eve didn't have all of these other conditions to blame for their actions. They were the first. Their only experience was the good life before Snake came along. Their frame of reference was only the life they lived before they ate the apple. They must have liked the good life, because that was what they wanted back. They didn't want the trouble that Snake had caused. Opps! There we go again, blaming Snake.

The foundation from which mankind was created was so sound that even in a state of turmoil when Eve chose the apple and was caught red handed (or with her hand in the cookie jar so to speak), she chose to try and stay in God's good graces. That foundation was in fact the only foundation that Adam and Eve had experienced, God's unending love. After all, even though he threw them out of the Garden, he did sew clothes for them[11]. God's wrath was experienced for certain but, they had the backbone to stand up to God's punishment and didn't go slithering off. The framework of existence that surrounded them was sound enough that they knew where to go to receive the comfort they needed to continue with their existence. They chose to try to recreate that "good life". We tend to consider recreation differently today.

God was worried, however. Look at Genesis 3 vs 22 again. "Then the Lord God said, 'The man has become like one of us; he knows good and evil. We must keep him from eating some of the fruit from the tree of life, or he will live forever'". But that is a subject for a whole other book.

We have the same options as Snake every time we are tempted. So why does Snake choose to be a snake and why do we continue to think we can be part time snakes? Snake wants a second chance to take advantage of us. On the other hand, we keep finding that through God's grace we get second chances to be the creation He intended us to be. For some reason, the cycle continues to repeat itself. We continue to ignore the framework that God has given us to exist without bowing to temptation. Snakes are still there. The temptations are still there. The choices are still there. The habits are still there. AND, we still think we can sneak one past. What conniving creatures we are! God forgive us! PLEASE!

REFERENCES

1. Mathew: Chapter 4
2. Bernard Madoff, 71, was sentenced in June of 2009 to 150 years in prison for orchestrating a massive Ponzi scheme that spanned decades and spun a web of phantom wealth.
3. Genesis 3:5
4. Genesis 3:6
5. Genesis 3:10
6. Genesis 3:7
7. Genesis 3:16
8. Genesis 3:19
9. Genesis 3:23
10. Genesis 3:12
11. Genesis 3:21
12. "The Silence Of Adam", Dr. Larry Crabb, Zandervan, Grand Raids, MI, 1995

DISCUSSIONS QUESTIONS

1. How do you deal with temptation?
2. When was the last time you were a victim of temptation?
3. How did you feel after being tempted?

THE SNAKE

CHAPTER 7

**To Bite Or Not To Bite,
That Is The Question!
What Is It About Temptation?**

*When it is decision time, we always wonder
If what we decide will put us under!*

Visualize the most magnificent garden – lush, moist with the morning dew, plants too many to count…oh to be a Master Gardener! Paradise flourishing from the waters of four major rivers, Pishon, Gihon, Tigris, and Euphrates giving life to all these remarkable species of flora[1]. No doubt that Adam and Eve were in paradise. If you read Genesis Chapter 3 with a digging effort, you might say they were in eternal paradise.

Visualize still further as the Master Groundskeeper in this luscious paradise garden approaches you and asks you to start naming every plant, tree, shrub, and bush. What an honor! As you look around you can just feel the excitement growing as you think about this awesome task.

The excitement must show on your face as the Master Groundskeeper takes full advantage of this opportunity and he tells you "When you are done with the first task, I want you to name all the beasts of the earth and the birds of the air"[2]. Talk about an awesome overwhelming task! What great trust the Master Groundskeeper has put in you. As you look around with all of these good feelings weighing on your mind, excitement sets in and then one devastating thought comes to mind, where would you begin?

In Ancient Near Eastern culture, to name something, and sometimes just to know a name, is a sign of authority. Often times it is authority over or at least an approaching of equality. That is why the demons demonstrate their knowledge of Jesus as the "Son of God"[3] and also why he asks what the demons names are i.e. "legion, for we are many"[4]. Here, Adam is represented as having authority over the animals by being the one who names them. This isn't completely unfamiliar in our culture, in that we name our children and they are stuck with that name until they are of age to change it if they so desire.

After assigning these tasks, the Master Groundskeeper takes his leave, but before He departs He turns and says a strange thing completely out of context with this fantastic obligation he has just given you, "You may freely eat the fruit of every tree in the garden except the tree of the knowledge of good and evil. If you eat its fruit, you are sure to die."[5] With all of the freedom he has just given you and the tasks he wanted you to do, now he gives you a "DON'T DO". Your mind is swirling with excitement about being able to name anything whatever you want, and being able to eat anything you want, now there are restraints. What gives any way?

Off you go, note pad and Sharpie in hand, excitement in your heart, looking for a place to begin. You wander the garden, but cannot stop thinking about what the Master Groundskeeper told you "You may freely eat the fruit of every tree in the garden except the tree of the knowledge of good and evil. If you eat its fruit, you are sure to die."[5] Why would Master set me to a task of naming everything and at the same time tell me to stay away from this one tree? Not only that, He asked you to name everything, but he has already named this tree, "The Tree Of Knowledge of Good and Evil". What kind of name is that? Knowledge of Good and Evil, you don't even know what that means, let alone have a desire to eat the fruit. Does the Master Groundskeeper know what that means? Other questions begin to go through your mind, like why is only this one forbidden? Is it just because the Master Groundskeeper says so? What does he know that I don't know?

Isn't it strange how our minds won't let loose of nagging thoughts like this! We know what we have been told but we just can't concentrate on the task at hand because of those little distracting temptations. Even if we confront the temptation, we still have to make a conscious effort to avoid it. Old clichés like a dog with a bone and taking candy from a baby come to mind. But once someone says no, we immediately wonder why. Most of the time, we can ignore these temptations. In fact Adam managed to ignore the temptation for quite some time. He probably was able to complete most of his assigned task without giving the forbidden tree a second thought. He stuck with simple names like oak, maple, sycamore, daffodil, tulip, dandelion, etc, but his mind kept coming back to that tree named The Tree of Knowledge of Good and Evil.

"So what is the big deal about this tree any way?" Adam began his task diligently, but all he could think about was that TREE! His curiosity probably drew him toward the TREE like a magnet. Each time he approached the TREE he noticed a light misty fog enveloping the TREE. He couldn't help but wonder about the strangeness of the TREE, but also, he couldn't help but remember the master groundskeeper's warning "You may freely eat the fruit of every tree in the garden except the tree of the knowledge of good and evil. If you eat its fruit, you are sure to die."[3] Somehow Adam knew he had to respect his elders, so off he went to finish the task at hand with his Sharpie and notepad; cow, pig, blue jay, robin, and the serpent!

It is interesting that Adam completed most of this first task without having the companionship of Eve. In this account, God created Eve after the Master Groundskeeper had brought all of the animals to Adam to be named[6]. It was Eve who carried the curiosity to its conclusion, but Adam's curiosity wasn't far behind. While Adam spent quite some time naming everything and managed to avoid the temptation but Eve apparently only had Snake to distract her and Snake wasn't about to allow any sidetrack from this opportunity. It was curious as well and being as shrewd as it was, Snake saw a cleaver way to entice Eve to decide to give in to the temptation.

Snake's decision-making process required significant contemplation. After all, Eve was living in paradise and had no real reason to go against what the Master Groundskeeper had told them. You can just see her agonizing over this temptation and the decision to do something she had heard about. The Master Groundskeeper hadn't told her directly not to eat the fruit from the tree of knowledge of good and evil. In fact, Snake took advantage of this aspect when he said "did God really say you must not eat fruit from any tree in the garden?"[7]

Eve's response was not exactly what the Master Groundskeeper had said. Her answer helps us understand that she had been thinking about the issue before Snake even came around. Eve added that "you must not even touch the tree"[8] or you will surely die. The difference between touching and eating may not be significant, but she must have been thinking about this "opportunity" for some time. Adam must have told her about not eating the fruit from this tree but, we don't know for certain. Had they experienced death yet? If she had thought about this matter far enough, not eating the fruit might have meant that they wouldn't die. That is the problem with the decision making process, we tend to concentrate on what we believe are the benefits of the decision rather that the negative aspects. Sooner or later, we manage to talk ourselves into following what we know is the wrong path. The temptation and the decision! Sounds like a book title!

It wasn't enough to be the first botanist ever. There Adam was, the first human of Creation, in paradise with nothing to want and God decides out of all the potential sins that mankind will ever face, to put temptation first. God created us in His image. He is the Father and we must listen to his commands. Why did God place humans in the path of temptation? More specifically, why did God choose this particular temptation; knowledge of good and evil? Plenty of other choices existed. Consider the three temptations of Christ for example; food; all the kingdoms of the world; and being left in the hands of angels. Christ would have nothing to do with any of them.[9]

Temptations always exist. Adam lived with this particular temptation for a fairly long time. He knew about the tree of knowledge of good and evil right from his first day in the Garden. What was it about this temptation that caused Adam to give in to the offering? Was the decision to explore this first temptation made because after God created woman Adam was not alone? Perhaps; but the tree of life was right next to the tree of knowledge of good and evil[10], why was the fruit from the tree of life not chosen to be the forbidden fruit? After all, having the ability to live forever seems like a very worthwhile temptation.

Take this a step further; if Adam were the only human in existence, would knowledge of good and evil have any benefit? If he were the only human, the only way knowledge of good and evil would have any use would be to go against this Master Groundskeeper's direction. Maybe the Master Groundskeeper was thinking this very thought when he directed Adam not to eat this particular fruit. As soon as two people existed, the ability to differentiate between good and evil became an important issue that required mankind to decide whom he was going to follow, the Master Groundskeeper (God), or humans.

Since God knows all things, he knew that mankind would wrestle with the dilemma of following humans or God, again, and again, and again, and again. The story of Jesus being tempted three times by the devil mentioned above is in Matthew's Gospel[9] Three temptations by the devil and three times Jesus rebuked the devil. Snake was at work. Giving in to temptation and deciding to take the human side of the issue is a flaw we all possess, but not the Son of God. Jesus knew the story of the Garden of Eden and he was not going to disappoint his Father like His first creation had done. The chapter in Mathew is also about the decision that Jesus made to do God's will and not to give in to the temptations of the devil seeking worldly opportunities to become what man was expecting the messiah to become.

The bible has many other temptation lessons. Christ, for example, taught his followers to pray "And lead us not into temptation, but deliver us from the evil one."[11] God knows we lack self-control. "No temptation has seized you except what is common to man. And God is faithful; He will not let you be tempted beyond what you can bear. But when you are tempted, he will also provide a way out so that you can stand up under it."[12] God provides a way out; a powerful and incredible testimony from the Apostle Paul.

Adam and Eve, the first humans to be tempted, were given a way out as well. The Lord God told Adam "You may freely eat the fruit of every tree in the garden except the tree of the knowledge of good and evil. If you eat its fruit, you are sure to die."[5] Some translations say "instantly die". God is merciful and when he discovered He had been disobeyed, there were consequence[13], but they didn't instantly die. In fact, Adam lived to be 930 years old.[14] The point is however, Adam and his descendents didn't live eternally.

Temptation comes to us all![15] There is no escape! To bite or not to bite the forbidden fruit, that was the question (and still is). Temptations require decisions. We decide to satisfy our curiosity and we justify this decision with all manner of rationalization. Any excuse becomes a good excuse as we contemplate whether to give in to the temptation or not. We can use our temptations to become humbled and purified.[16] Jesus taught us that prayer is our solution to overcoming temptation. Yet, the temptations still lead us astray and our decisions to follow the temptations continue to deliver us into evil. You would think that we would know better by now. Solomon says that there is nothing new here on earth.[17] I guess he is right!

REFERENCE:

1. Genesis 2:10-14
2. Genesis 2:19
3. Mark 5:7
4. Mark 5:9
5. Genesis 2:16-17
6. Genesis 2:22
7. Genesis 3:1
8. Genesis 3:3 historically, this difference is not considered significant. The author has chosen to use the difference for illustration purposes.
9. Matthew 4
10. Genesis 2:9
11. Matthew 6:13
12. 1 Corinthians 10:13
13. Genesis 3:16-19
14. Genesis 5: 5
15. James 1:13
16. James 4:7-10
17. Ecclesiastes 1:9

DISCUSSION QUESTIONS

1. The Lord's Prayer (Matthew Chapter Six, Verse 13) reads "Lead us not into temptation, but deliver us from evil." Do you find comfort in Jesus' words?
2. Does prayer help you resist temptation?
3. Psalm 23:3 reads, "He leads me on paths of righteousness." Are you on the right path?

THE APPLE

CHAPTER 8

Can You Pick A Color….Any Color? Are You A Red Or A Golden Delicious, Or A Sour Granny Smith?

Will St. Peter at his gate
Decide your final state?

Eve took a bite of the fruit from the tree of knowledge and learned the difference between good and evil. This knowledge forever changed the relationship between man and God. The implications of that historic event are so far reaching, they are nearly impossible to imagine. But, let's imagine them anyway. Think about all that was involved. Eve was in paradise. She had no experience with being anywhere else. She didn't know anybody except Adam and God. She pretty much did as she pleased. She could go anywhere in her known universe and didn't really have to do anything for anybody. She was truly a free will and free spirited woman.

Why, then, with all the benefits of living in the garden did she think she needed to change this perfect living condition? She had it made as they say. But, once Eve met Snake, things changed. She knew that she wasn't supposed to take that bite. Here was a new experience for her, another creature to talk to.

Imagine her standing there in all of her natural beauty casually talking with Snake. The only thing they had in common was the garden. So probably, their conversation was about what was going on in the garden.

"Hi Snake, how you doing this morning? Adam is off with his notepad and Sharpie naming more of the flora. What have you been up to?"

Snake, being the subtle creature that it was, wouldn't come right out and tell her that it was up to no good. After all Snake was a deceitful creature. So what does it do? It says, "You know, Eve, its good to have a creature like you in the garden. Your natural beauty brings a new dimension to the rest of us creatures. I have been admiring you as you have walked around. God did well when He created you."

"Well, thanks Snake. It is kind of you to notice," said Eve. Now subtle Snake has set the stage. It has Eve thinking about other things she has not considered before, like her appearance and how she looks to other creatures.

So, Snake sets out more bait, "I think you are a lot smarter than Adam. But you know what? God was lying about the fruit in this here tree. If you eat it, it won't kill you like God said. No, it will, however, make you as smart as God."

Eve must have been very naive, or at least we would like to think that because nobody that inexperienced could possibly have fallen for a line like that without having something to compare it to. But there she was standing in all of this natural beauty of hers looking right at Snake, listening to this hog wash and she takes the bait, hook, line, and sinker. She couldn't let this new-found companion think she was an air head. Her pride was just created.

Her feeble attempt to brush Snake away and keep on the good side of God was equally disconcerting. "But God said we mustn't eat that fruit." Ya, right! That really convinced Snake!

Before Eve could indulge herself with that first bite, however, she must have thought about the situation with some reservations. In her heart, she knew that what she was about to do was not in keeping with the instructions that God had given her and Adam. She knew it wasn't right. Somehow, however, in her mind she had justified that choice and she went ahead and did it. Maybe she had no reservations at all. However, it is a lot more fun visualizing her consternation.

The Bible doesn't tell us whether or not Adam has gotten to this tree with his notepad and Sharpie yet. We in our wisdom have equated that fruit from the tree of knowledge about good and evil to the apple. However, Genesis doesn't say the fruit was an apple. In keeping with that tradition, however, let's assume that Adam with his notepad and his Sharpie has made it far enough into the garden to name the fruit from this tree "apple".

Along comes Eve and Snake issues the temptation. As she ponders the choice between biting or not biting, she realizes that she doesn't know which "apple" to select. Genesis doesn't tell us that Snake handed her the fruit. So, unless the tree only had one apple, she had to make another choice. Not only was she about to defy God, she also had to consider which of the "apples" to choose to accomplish the task. My, oh my, what thoughts can you visualize going through her head? Some how, since she was choosing to defy God, she looses track of the big picture and finds herself caught up in the task of making a mundane choice about which of the apples to bite. Little did she know that what she was about to do would result in an eternity of making choices.

God probably didn't make this choice easy. As soon as Eve chose to defy God, the actual act would require additional judgments on her part. What criteria did she use to select this apple for this first defiant act? What basis did she have to make the selection? After all, she was new at this defiant stuff and neither her nor Adam had any previous defying experiences. Of course, she had all of her senses, so appearance, smell, and touch would all come into play. Not having eaten an apple before, taste would not be an issue. But she probably knew that taste and smell were related. Imagine her standing there trying to choose the first fruit to bite.

Having Eve trying to make a choice about which apple to eat congers up all kinds of cartoon like visions. Of course, these visions completely take away from the actual act itself. Once mankind was given the freedom of choice, the act of exploiting that freedom began immediately as Eve contemplated which apple to bit. We have never managed to overcome the agony of making the proper choice. As I think about this, the vision of going shoe shopping with my wife comes to mind. My wife never seems to be able to find shoes she likes. But that is another story. Since I now know better than to make a choice for her, just let it be said that I will never pick out another pair of shoes that I think she might like. I wonder if Eve let Snake pick out the apple for her.

Other cartoons about that first defiant act, freedom of choice, and the consternation that exists with that freedom abound. For example, The South Bend Tribune on May 8, 2007 had a Mother Goose & Grimm cartoon showing Eve handing Adam a bowl of fruit saying "I hope you like it… it's forbidden fruit salad"[3]. Again, we make fun of the fact that God gave us the freedom of choice but we don't seem to know how to make the choice freely.

Maybe, since it was God's garden, one would think that the apples were so perfect that it didn't matter which one she selected. Maybe they were all the same. No misshapen fruit, no ripe on one side and green on the other, no worms, no "drops", nothing to distract Eve from participating in this historical defiant act. Somehow, I don't believe that was the case. In God's unique way, I would guess that His perspective about perfection does not include these aspects.

With the apple selections we have today, would she select on the basis of size, or the basis of color, or the basis of aroma or some other selection criteria. In our experience, we know she wouldn't select a bruised one or one with a worm hole unless she had no other choice and really wanted an apple. We know that if she had a choice, she wouldn't select a misshapen one. As long as she was going to defy God, was she going to take the biggest and best looking apple she could find! The more I think about this first defiant act, I can't help but relate this process to all the opportunities we have to defy God's trust in our use of his God given talents. No matter what choice we make, it seems that a better choice is available if we would only think about the matter a little more. But hindsight is 20-20 as they say.

Eve was probably no different in this first defiant act. The moment she chose to defy God was the moment that her mind went to work justifying her defiance and reasoning out how right this act was. In that moment of decision, she knew in her heart that God was not going to like her action. Yet, she went ahead and did it anyway. She recognized that her act was only righteous in her mind and she knew that no matter how she justified it, God wasn't going to like it. She knew it!

Justification and righteousness, as I understand, come from the same Greek root word[1]. They also come from the same Hebrew root word[2]. Contemplating and discussing the meaning of these two words can be argumentative confusing, misinterpretive, and self-serving depending on your perspective or whomever you are trying to convince, and what you are trying to achieve. However, I have found that once you include atonement, all of the arguments seem to melt away. From then on, justifying evil as good and making it right with God has been a forever mankind problem that only atonement can truly achieve.

We all know when our acts are in defiance of God's will. We know the difference between good and evil. We try to justify some of our actions by reasoning that we selected the lesser of two evils. It doesn't matter how red the apple was, eating the damn thing was wrong! It doesn't matter how wrong our act was, it was wrong.

REFERENCES

1. Justified in Greek is dikaioo, and Righteous in Greek is dikaios both from the root dikaios

2. Justified in Hebrew is tsaddiyq, and righteous in Hebrew is tsedaqah both from the root tsadaq

3. Mother Goose and Grimm is an internationally syndicated comic strip by Pulitzer Prize-winning cartoonist Mike Peters. It was first syndicated in 1984 and is distributed by King Features Syndicate.

DISCUSSION QUESTIONS

1. Good and evil have always existed. Have you handled your <u>knowledge</u> of the difference between the two acceptably to your satisfaction?

2. Obsessions can influence relationships. Do you seek friends with the same obsessions you have? How has that choice helped you grow spiritually/

3. Do you think your knowledge of good and evil will get in the way of experiencing eternal life?

THE APPLE

CHAPTER 9

How Big Of A Bite Can You Take?

We are glutens for punishment|
But what we need is His nourishment!

I have never thought about this before, but now that I am, I have to wonder, what did Eve "see" the moment that she took that first bite. Her awareness of her surroundings must have given her a whole new meaning, a whole new vista. And then you have to wonder about the state of mind that followed. Was she excited? Was she awed? Was her breath taken away? Was her mind overloaded with all of the possibilities at her fingertips so to speak? Was she humiliated? Was she stunned at the realization that her choices had consequences? Did she have choices that were never considered before? And then, you have to wonder, did she want to take a bigger bite or did she want to spit out the bite she took. In any event, it was too late to do anything except to eat.

For the last four years I have taken a fishing trip to Ontario, Canada. We fish for a week at a remote fly-in lake. Ontario has strict laws about what fish you can keep, and we are required to sort what we catch. Only so many fish can be kept and they have to be bigger than a minimum and smaller than a maximum. As a consequence, many of the fish that we catch are released. That is not a bad thing, but we have often talked about what could possibly go through the released fish's mind. Here the fish is just swimming along trying to find something to satisfy its hunger when all of a sudden it bites a "food" that drags it off to a world that it has never seen before. It is lifted out of the water and sees creatures that it has never experienced and for an instant it is handled and is suddenly returned to the environment where it had lived all of its life. Can't you just see that fish wondering about what just happened? I can imagine that Eve had the same experience and just like the fish, when she was put back into her original environment wondering what had just happened to her. She now viewed her environment differently.

Eve's mental awareness of her surroundings must have taken on an entirely different aura. I think all of us can visualize her reaction. We all have experienced occasions when our minds comprehend that our actions have caused an opportunity that we had neither considered nor planned. We know our actions will result in consequences. We know our situations will result in choices, and we know that our choices could lead to mental manipulations of what is right and what is wrong.

Eve must have experienced the same things, but one difference existed, this was the first time ever. She had no prior experience with this situation and had no comprehension of what she was supposed to do. Obviously, she didn't spit it out. It definitely was too late once she took that bite. The vista that lay before her was probably a mish-mash of choices that involved all that we worry about as we go through life. Not only the basic concerns regarding preservation but relationships as well. Keep in mind that up until that bite, Eve had everything provided and the only relationships were with God, Adam, and that snake, which was now slithering away with a chuckle. But just the same, I can imagine that life in her mind became a complicated maze of choices. Maybe she thought that a second bite would clarify everything, so she had Adam take the bite. Nope! That didn't help! In fact, the situation only got worse. Once the act was completed, there was no turning back. There was no way to make it right. The only choice left was to go on and hope that somehow a right relationship with God could be reformed, recreated.

We all know what we would do if we found a penny lying on the sidewalk. Some of us would pick it up and put it in our pocket.

Others would pick it up and put it in their shoe for good luck. Still others would ignore it because it was only a penny. However, none of us would try to find the real owner. But what if instead of a penny, a billfold containing $800.00 was the object laying on the sidewalk? Suddenly, we have choices. We can leave it there. But we know that someone will find it just as we did. We can pick it up and keep what we want. After all, finder's keepers, loser's weepers, right? Or we can try to find the real owners. Even then, we don't know what to do if the real owner isn't found or if we don't try hard enough or if we give it to the authorities and they don't really try. Our minds really work overtime don't they? And the justification exercises kick in. But just like Eve, in the end, it comes down to what is between God and us. It comes down to what in our heart we believe is the right thing to do. We may not do what is right, but that is what it comes down to. When the real owner is found, imagine the elation on all sides!

Eve may not have realized all of the ramifications of taking that first bite, but in her heart I would wager she had an inkling that the moment she took that bite, she was changing a relationship. She had an inkling her defiance of God was putting her self before God. She had an inkling the only way she could go was to take Adam with her otherwise she was going to be alone. She had an inkling she couldn't experience what ever it was that she wanted to experience without taking that bite. She had an inkling if she didn't take that bite when she took it, she was going to take that bite sometime. She had an inkling she was going to defy God. In her mind, she had to eventually.

I wonder how long she struggled with the notion that she needed to take that bite. It doesn't matter. As long as she didn't bite the apple, even if she had it in her mind that she needed to take that bite and didn't, she was obeying God. At least that is how she justified not taking the bite. That apple had become an obsession. From the very beginning, she knew that biting the apple was in defiance of God. This knowledge alone was getting in the way of having the perfect relationship with God.

Eve had already ruined the perfect relationship with God simply by considering the bite in the first place. But that was nothing like the actual act. To Eve, that must have been the most delicious tasting bite she had ever taken of any of God's creations. She must have thought her act was the greatest thing since God breathed life into her body. She must have felt such exhilaration that couldn't help but want more. She, she, she, she!!!!!!!!

No doubt about it, Eve had a life changing experience. The moment she took that first bite, the inkling went away and she knew that she had defied God. She knew before she took that bite, defying God was going to happen; but she had no idea what would be the consequences. Her mind couldn't have been prepared for the changes that occurred. We know that something must have happened, because she did at least two things immediately after the experience. She got Adam to try the apple and they covered themselves with fig leaf aprons. Then they hid!

The question now became what do they do about it? How do they let this new experience influence their lives? A moment before Eve took that first bite, she was contemplating which of the apples to bite, never anticipating that the action would cause such a dramatic change in her life. All of a sudden, she realized that she knew more than she thought she did. All of a sudden she realized that not everything was good. Now she also saw that a dark side existed with every experience she has. Not only that, she also realized that she couldn't ignore the dark side. The consequences of any action on her part would now influence any and every action she took in the future.

Holy molly! What an awesome realization! I have to admit, my mind has me wanting to take a bigger bite just to experience more of this new understanding. No wonder God kicked them out of the garden and kept them from eating the fruit of the tree of life. Nothing like having all of this knowledge and living forever!

One has to wonder if the reason we have to die comes from the extreme danger of having this knowledge and also lining forever.

Death at least brings an end! Think about it when a tyrant dies, there may be change. Perhaps this is why there is still and "end time". God has to wrap it up or it will become overwhelmingly devastating, going from worse to worse.

That first look into the difference between good and evil must have generated a vista of a complicated intertwining maze. After having nothing but a perfect relationship with God, I can imagine the confusion that resulted. Although having a perfect relationship with God is not in my experience, being in the presence of good and evil has generated a lifetime of experiences that still confounds me. Evil has a way of camouflaging itself into such delightful indulgences. Sometimes, the evil of the situation does not come into view until it is too late. Sometimes we see the evil and do it anyway. Sometimes the evil and good are not easily separated and we need to make complicated choices.

I can't help but wonder if God experiences these same confounding choices. When I read the Old Testament, I get confused with what God tells his chosen people to do; what he will do; what the chosen people really do; and what God really does. How does He know which choice is the "perfect" choice especially when His chosen people decide not to follow His directions or when they complain about the direction that He has selected for them?

I am certain that He is aware of more choices than I am. My mind is limited by "what is in it for me" but God has no such limitations. He can see all of the possibilities, where I can't. He knows what will happen with each choice. But He gave us free will. Does He know what we will choose? Enough about choices! My head hurts just thinking about it. This reminds me about an e-mail I received from a friend that sends me a thought for the day. I don't know the source, but the e-mail I received referenced Ezra Taft Benson who reportedly said, "Pride is concerned with who is right. Humility is concerned with what is right."

The vista that Eve saw with that first bite wasn't repelling. It couldn't have been because we know that she got Adam to take a bite as well.

She didn't spit it out, so it must have tasted ok. Let's imagine that she experienced nothing except the guilt feeling for defying God! She didn't die! Lightening didn't strike. What she knew didn't change. The only sensation was that the realization that she had satisfied her hunger. All of these expectations and nothing happened! What a disappointment. Then again, maybe it wasn't a disappointment!

She knew that what she experienced changed her. She knew that her actions were not right. She had taken a step that altered the relationship she had with God and probably with Adam. The change was one that was not easy to explain. She thought that she was going to experience something profound and got nothing. But, God knew, God knew that the change was for ever and that the change was devastating. God knew that her defiance was only the first step in the process of questioning the relationship that He wanted with man. He knew that man would have to figure it out on his own.

Eve must have considered the experience of that first bite as being frustrating. Compared to her expectations, did she get what she wanted? Did she get what Snake said she would get? She had one thing in mind and instead got something else. In today's experience, it would be like putting a new program into a computer (sort of). She got what you wanted to a certain extent but a whole lot of unwanted peripherals came with it. The major difference is that she couldn't remove the program. She was stuck with it. And the snake had her e-mail address. Let the garbage sorting begin.

DISCUSSION QUESTIONS

1. We have all been caught doing something defiant. How did you justify you actions? Lies or truth?

2. We all have disappointed GOD or someone we love. What did you do next?

3. If you took the time to visualize the consequences of your actions, would you make better decisions?

THE KNOWLEDGE

CHAPTER 10

Can You Imagine What It Would Have Been Like (If Eve Hadn't Eaten The Apple)?

Thinking about the relationship with God
Not knowing evil is odd!

It is not too much to expect perfection. However, expectations and reality are two different things. Perfection is rarely achieved without some controversy. In a few instances, like bowling, achievement of perfection can not be disputed. Most often, the achievement is highly disputed. As a matter of fact, the desire to achieve perfection is the source of considerable anguish. This anguish is mostly on the part of the "expector" rather than on the part of the "expectee". The automotive industry, for example expects scrap rates to be in the parts per billion. Yet in some industries that supply parts to the automotive industry, reducing scrap from 40% to 5% is a major accomplishment. (Just in case you are wondering, 5% is 5 parts per 100 and 1 part per billion is 0.0000001%.) Our expectations of perfection lead to much consternation. We expect others to live up to our vision of perfection while at the same time we accept less than perfection for ourselves. Memory is very convenient. We seem to forgive and forget the things we've done, but have a much more difficult time forgiving and forgetting the things we feel others have done to us. Thanks to Eve, achieving that perfect relationship with God requires considerably more work than it originally did in the Garden of Eden.

I have an acquaintance who works for the highway department in Illinois. On occasion, I have met him in the middle of the afternoon at a key club where we are members. Membership permitted us to go behind the bar and fix ourselves a drink or two (or three). Those middle of the afternoon occasions were usually filled with lamenting about the rest of the world. He used to say that a man can only stand just so much stupidity in a given time and then he has to leave. That was his excuse for having a drink in the middle of the afternoon. I don't remember what my excuse was. His feelings on those occasions illustrate how judgmental we are. Like we are the smartest people in the world and our way has no competition! Ya right about that one too! Thanks, Eve, for allowing us to believe that God handed out brains to a select few.

Our vast experience leads us to the half vast notion that our way is the only way to perfection. We can't help but believe that any action, other than the one that we can visualize, will lead to dire consequences. Our fears are based on the facts that we believe; we know evil when we see it; we know that the path to success is a perfect trail; yet that trail is filled with potholes just waiting for us to trip over. We can see some of the potholes because we have already fallen into them or at least considered them, are aware they exist. What's more is that we can't understand why others don't have the vision and wisdom that we do. I mean if we can see them, why can't others see them? Eve some how managed to have us believe we know it all, probably because she took the first bite.

Perfection has many sides. Each of us has a view of perfection and frequently we believe our view is best for everyone. Thus, we are persistent about trying to convince others that our view is best for them. If they don't see our side, we think they are shortsighted. We think they are stubborn. We think they have ulterior motives. We think they have lost their common sense. We think they are selfish. We think they lack ambition (or have too much ambition). Eve's view of perfection was that she could know as much as God, at least that is what Snake taught her[1].

The church where we are members is in a small Midwest conservative community where change takes place at a rate equivalent to a glacier moving and is not experienced without misunderstandings and hurt feelings. Sudden changes or changes of significant magnitude will not happen without a collective accommodation or without someone becoming convinced that the changes were personally directed towards them.

In the particular instance that comes to mind, a progressive set of members wanted to increase church attendance by changing the way the community viewed the Sunday gathering of believers particularly for the early Sunday morning service where a contemporary worship style was utilized. They proposed the opportunity to bring coffee into the sanctuary for the contemporary worship service. The contemporary worship had already caused a rift with the other members due to declining participation in the traditional worship. In the minds of some, the congregation had become divided. Certain members became very irate over the degradation that coffee drinking caused to their concept of worship. The hullabaloo that the coffee clash caused was so out of proportion to the congregation's desire to reach out to the community that the church became a beacon of laughter in the community. A resolution was passed that coffee would not be permitted in the sanctuary during worship. Thankfully, the resolution did not designate who the coffee police would be and no penalties were to be imposed if one would get caught with a cup of coffee in the sanctuary. But, the situation caused the loss of the hard working support of several key church members and those who did not want coffee in the sanctuary still have not stepped up to fill in the gaps that resulted. Thanks, Eve, controversy over what is right and what is wrong will never go away.

So where were the good and evil in this situation? They were all within the minds of the individuals, me included. The perfect path was never revealed. Our shortsighted individualistic view of right and wrong got in the way of rationally dealing with a real life situation over practically nothing. You would think that we have better things to do than to make a commotion about a lousy cup of coffee. If we could only put this kind of emotion into dealing with real problems, we might be able to make some progress toward that perfect world that God intended before we learned that good and evil had a difference. Eve, what have you done? I understand that some churches even have Starbucks these days.

Ayn Rand in her book "Atlas Shrugged" paints a picture of people conflicted when one group demands that all of us owe it to each other to give their God given talents to the rest of the world[2]. The other group demands to be compensated for their talents before they give them to the rest of the world. Rand's point is two fold. First, if we withhold our talents, the world as most of us know it will fall apart. Secondly, if we give our talents freely, we take away the incentive for others to work for what they get. If we consider the background from which Ms Rand writes her book, much of this makes sense. She came from Russia immediately after the Bolshevik revolution. Communism, in her mind and I guess in most of our minds, is based on need. If you need it, you can have it; and if you have it you need to give it. Fortunately, Eve had nothing to do with this. (I am not trying to take away from those who work hard in a socialistic society, where ideally this concept would work. However, I am pointing out the realistic fact that the incentive for sharing has its advantages and disadvantages depending on who benefits from the sharing.)

As I read "Atlas Shrugged", I had difficulty justifying what I believed as a Christian and the ideas that Ms Rand was teaching. To me her ideas made sense, but for some reason, they conflicted with my Christian beliefs. I still have difficulties bringing these two rationalizations together. But I still believe both. Her ideas would work only if **everyone** was willing to share their God given talents with each other and **no one** thought that they deserved the results of the talents of others. Eve's selfish act made it impossible for this dilemma to be solved.

Right and wrong; good and evil; freedom of choice; perfection between man and God are all intertwined with that first act of defiance. God had more in store for us when He created us than to be wandering the garden with our notepad and Sharpie naming the fauna and flora. But there are times when we have lost track of what that was. So what is it that we have lost track of?

The world without knowledge of good and evil, without knowledge of right and wrong, without freedom of choice has one thing in common with the world where all of these issues exist and we have lost track of it. It would be great if we could exist in a world where people don't think of themselves first, but we don't. Eve took care of that. (Some would say that I might be a little hard on Eve. I really do like women. After all, Eve did share her new found vision when she invited Adam to take a bite as well. Adam did have a choice too!)

I have a close personal friend who finds it difficult to accept a free lunch. I have been with him when he refused to eat a supper that was prepared by my son and his family because in his mind he had not contributed anything toward the meal. Of course, he was kind enough to simply indicate he wasn't hungry, but in actuality, he had chosen not to accept the offering because it was something for nothing. He had failed to acknowledge that his friendship at the table was good enough. He had failed to acknowledge that we have to leave enough room for others to give as well. You see, my friend would more than willingly give you all that he had if you wanted it. He takes great joy in giving what he has to others. But, if he doesn't feel he has given enough of himself to warrant receiving something than he has difficulty accepting an unconditional gift. Thanks, Eve, for making us feel guilty about accepting something simply for the love of God.

This same friend was really upset with his daughter when her church family helped her family through a financial difficulty. He was upset because he had thought that he had taught her more about how to say thank you when some one helped without being asked. He was embarrassed by her actions and took it personally as a reflection on him. Fortunately, his daughter did say thank you, but I don't know if it was because he said something or if it was because of a true act of thankfulness that came from her as the result of the right and wrong he had taught her. In any event, Eve, thanks for the embarrassment that we feel when we think that we are guilty of inadequately teaching our children the difference between right and wrong.

We could go on and on with these examples because we have forgotten about what God has in store for us. The world without knowledge of good and evil, without knowledge of right and wrong, the world without freedom of choice has one thing in common with the world that exists because Eve took an apple break. But, we have forgotten it!

We get caught up in those issues which we think are important like give, give, give or take, take, take. We get caught up in our expectations of others without giving thought to what God expects of us. We develop expectations of others and when they fail to live up to our expectations, we find them guilty of our imagined wrong. We blame them for not adequately seeing what we think is the big picture like we know it all. We have not taken the log out of our eye! There does have to be a big picture though, doesn't there? Jesus summed it up in saying "Love the Lord your God with all your heart, soul, and mind and love your neighbor as yourself. Do this and you will fulfill all of the requirements of the law and the prophets.[3]

We can't even get out of bed in the morning with out judging others. We have no idea what the world would be like without having some expectations of others. We can't help judging whether others have fulfilled our expectation because we think they have an ulterior motive.

This morning, I teased my wife about getting out of bed at 8:30am. (I had been up since 6:00am). However, no matter how I tried, she had no guilt feeling about sleeping in. She had no qualms about my remarks concerning how much the bed was missing her. Everything was right in her world. After all, we were on vacation. So what's my point, as they say! Our judgmental selves wouldn't exist without Eve.

Not only is there good and evil, right and wrong, but as I suggested in Chapter 2 God does not take the consequences. Although I am having a little fun blaming Eve, we all know that all of our choices have consequences and it didn't take Eve having an apple break to figure that out. We exist with the talents that God has given us. We depend on the talents of others to be able to effectively use our own talents. Yes, sometimes we wish that people had more common sense than they do and perhaps we are a little too hard on them and ourselves. But, we still have forgotten the one thing that matters most. We have made too many assumptions about what God expects of others. We have created our own image of what the perfect relationship with God is to be like. The boundaries that we have generated make assumptions about God that are not realistic.

So, if Eve hadn't eaten the apple, what would our world be like? What would the perfect relationship with God encompass? What would existence without choices accomplish? How can relationships with others exist without competition, without expectations, without jealousy, without judgmental issues? I can only imagine.

The opportunity for that perfect relationship with God still exists. But we need to be constantly reminded about our own limitations. We need to experience first hand that embarrassment of putting self first. We need to experience first hand that guilty feeling that we have not done God's will. We need to experience first hand the judgment of others with respect to the will of God. We need to be reminded that others have an equal opportunity to experience the freedom of choice that God had given each of us not just me. We need to hear the anguish of others when they explain their reasons for giving and for taking. We need to hear the frustration that others experience with our choices so that we can explore the opportunities to experience the kingdom of right relationships. Most of all, we need to relearn as often as possible and remember that all of the glory belongs to God the creator and that we are the created.

REFERENCES

1. Genesis 3:5
2. Random House October 10, 1957
3. Matthew 22: 37 – 40

DISCUSSION QUESTIONS

1. Why do some people give, while others take?
2. Are you selfish or generous?
3. Are you working on improving your relationship with GOD?

THE KNOWLEDGE

CHAPTER 11

How Much Knowledge (Good and Evil) Is There?

You know what I mean, you insist!
But to everything is given a twist.

Potentially, every situation has its dark side! Thankfully, every situation also has its bright side as well. Where we get into trouble is with the evil that goes along with the good and with the good that goes along with the evil. We can't seem to have just black and white. No matter how bright the choice, some one always seems to be around to get offended.

There are times when I seem to work my tail off doing what I think is right certain that I have gone about my business in such a manner that no one is offended. Just the same, low and behold, some one takes what I have done differently than I intended. At least that is what it seems like to me. When it comes to decorating, I can't pick the right color. When it comes to singing, I throw the rest of the choir off. When it comes to putting away the dishes, I have put them in the wrong place and someone needs to move them. When it comes to painting, I haven't put enough on in some places. When it comes to driving, I am not going fast enough for some people. The definition of a split second is the interval between the instant the light turns green and the guy behind me honks his horn. I just don't seem to get it right.

Of course on the other bright side of the plate, the view isn't the same. The color is ok but toning it down might be better. The music is ok but perhaps playing an instrument instead of singing would be better particularly with my ability to know one note from another when I am singing. As far as the dishes go, putting them away is ok but consideration of how and where they might be used next could prove beneficial. Applying the paint helps, but a second coat offers more protection. Although driving slow is ok in some situations, 40mph in a 70mph zone could be dangerous. And as far as red lights are concerned, being aware that others are in need of getting to their destination would cut down on aggravation. (You charter members of the ADL (Anti Destination League) ought to take note.)

Justifying evil with a self righteous attitude doesn't work either. Justifying good with a humble attitude is just as evil. If good was being done for good's sake, justifying wouldn't be necessary. Think about it! If we have to justify anything, evil was involved. If we have to make up and excuse, evil was involved. Good will stand on its own merit. Good does not require excuses. Good does not need a place to be camouflaged. Good does not need to be subtle. Good does not need to hide after it was performed. When anything is done for good, nothing can take away from it except evil. As soon as we point out the good in something, evil intent exists. Good is easily recognized on its own. It requires no champion. Even when good honors good, the evil is lurking in the background in the form of recognition. The perfect act of goodness is only with the doer. The goodness of the receiver requires nothing more that an acknowledgement of appreciation. Anything more is for some form of self gain and the evil steps in to be recognized. As we stated earlier, there is no such thing as a small evil. Evil is evil no matter how big or how small.

It is amazing how evil attacks even the youngest. I have a 5 year old nephew and a 3 year old niece. The other day while they were playing in the yard, the 5 year old nearly ran over his sister with his electric motorcycle. When he was confronted with the event by his grandmother, he indicated that it wasn't his fault because his sister had been the one that had gone in front of the toy. Accepting responsibility, putting the blame on others are all part of this knowledge of good and evil. I remember my son, who is now 42 years old, playing with his cousin when they were about 5 years old and getting caught pulling his cousin's hair. She had a lovely ponytail and as she was going up the steps from the basement he couldn't resist and he pulled the tail. When he was confronted with the "wrongness", he claimed her hair got caught in his fingers!

It is also amazing how evil can infiltrate our minds and ambitions. Evil can displace good in the blink of an eye. And to think we could have existed without any difference between good and evil if Eve hadn't taken that bite. Good goes unheralded while evil gets exalted. Good exists without notoriety, while evil takes all of the credit. Good is unspoken, while evil is a loud boisterous noise. Good goes unrecognized while evil gets all of the awards. Good exists without flare while evil is on all of the wanted posters. Good is special while evil is a plain burden to all that are around it. Good gets God's eternal acceptance while evil has no life beyond the moment.

Considering what has been written for this chapter might lead one to believe that our lives are full of nothing but evil. That belief is as far from the truth as possible. Most of the moments of our lives are filled with nothing but good. We don't think about it because that is the way good exists. We are happy to be content with the relationships as they are. No need to control them, no need to generate advantages, no need to have something better. These moments simply exist for the sake of goodness. These moments exists for the pure pleasure of the situation. We enjoy our families, we enjoy our friends, and we enjoy our opportunities because of the goodness that is there. Our happiest moments are those that require nothing from us except to be us.

Unfortunately, with evil lurking around, our happiest moments are the moments that we are most vulnerable to the rot that exists in the presence of evil. That is when evil with its subtle nature can sneak in and take advantage of the contentment that goes along with the presence of goodness. Enjoy your good self as often and as long as possible. Don't fear losing the goodness that is in your heart, because it cannot be replaced. It is there forever. The one major difference between good and evil is the satisfied sensation that goes along with the good experience. There is no way that evil can replace that sensation. Evil might fool you into thinking that it has a better lock on life, but when it really happens, the sour distasteful realization that evil has momentarily offset the good usually sets the experiences back on the right track.

For the most part no one intentionally sets out to be evil. We might get caught up in a situation where the dark side has taken advantage of a given set of circumstances, but most come to our senses with a good deal of guilt that what we have done is wrong. On rare occasions, those wrong moments come flooding back in our memories and we cringe to think about the consequences. On those occasions when the memories return, good has won out over evil but we are still paying the consequences. If a truly evil intent exists from the onset, it is rare and may God have mercy.

The goodness of creation exists all around us. We don't have to go far to experience the examples that God has left for us. Even in the violence of nature the goodness can be seen. Yes, sometimes we wonder at the destruction that occurs and how this all fits into the scheme of things, but by and large, we have to admit that the creator has endowed us with the beauty of goodness. In fact if we go back just two chapters in the book of Geneses[1], to the first story about creation in the bible, we find the definitions of good. I think the best definition was when God reached into darkness and pulled out light. Being able to see and understand the darkness goes a long way towards making everything good.

According to Frank Norris in his book **"The Octopus"**[2], darkness is the absence of light, and death is the absence of life. Carrying that notion one step further, a defect is the absence of perfection; and if we can, then, evil is the absence of good. God started his creation with good and the first seven days shows us how much good there really is[1].

If the definition of good at the beginning of Geneses isn't enough, God has also defined evil with His ten "shalt not's" in Exodus 20[3] and Deuteronomy 5[4]. The first three "shalt not's" spell out the goodness our creator expects in return for the goodness of His creation. Having no other gods, no graven images, and not taking His name in vain are straight forward responses with God to show your appreciation for the goodness of His creation. However, these same three commandments can be applied to interactions between all humans as well. The good that is in the relationships that result from these first three commandments between us humans and God and between all humans cannot be replaced with any form of evil. Following all of these commandments, and especially the first three commandments generates a relationship that is so unique, that nothing can detract from their good and their goodness.

Realizing that the good part of good and evil is all around us all of the time without pretense, prejudice, or the desire to be recognized generates a perfectly content regard for each other and for all of creation. Accepting "good" without pretense, without prejudice, and without honoring it seems to distract from the warm sensation that goes with it. As my wife taught me a long time ago, you don't have to make a big ado about it when someone gives you a complement, just simply say thank you. The same goes for this situation. So, God, accept our simple thank you from the goodness that is in our hearts.

REFERENCES

1. Genesis 1:18, 1:25, 1:31
2. **The Octopus,** by Frank Norris, Library Ed., Santa Ana, CA, Books on Tape Publisher 2000
3. Exodus 20:3 – 17
4. Deuteronomy 5:7 – 21

DISCUSSION QUESTIONS

1. When you are involved in a situation, do you try to be forthright and direct, or do you try to appease others?
2. Is a "little white lie" ok, or is it still evil?
3. Why do we think more about the evil things we have done, and less about the good things?

THE KNOWLEDGE

CHAPTER 12

How Can We Possibly Think That We Can Know As Much As The Creator?

God's creation included man in His plan.
So, man, don't recreate God in your plan.

Knowledge! Can we possibly imagine how much knowledge exists in this world? Just think about how much you know! Just think about how much you have learned! Just think about how much you have forgotten!

Just think about how much knowledge you use in your everyday life and you don't even need to know it. For example, we know what happens when we turn on a light switch, but do we know how it happens? Yes, I know, we don't need to know as long as the light comes on. But just think about all of that knowledge out there.

The television show, Jeopardy[4], amazes me. I occasionally get an answer (opps, I mean question) correct and sometimes I can even come up with the correct question when the other contestants didn't, but that is extremely rare. Where does all of this knowledge come from? I know we are not expected to know everything, but wow, some of those contestants really have a large knowledge bank! And then we add memory and recall. Some times the <u>answer</u> prods a memory and maybe I could come up with the <u>question</u> if I were give enough time.

Even memory makes me envious of some people. I have an acquaintance who can remember facts and figures that will astound most of us. Once he knows your name and vital statistics, he can recall them instantaneously. He does the same thing with baseball statistics. Memory and recall! How do they do it?

I guess it takes a desire to pick the knowledge that we want to remember. But yet, some people seem to have learned how to remember some facts that most of us complain about forgetting the moment after we are introduced, like the simple matter of a person's name, let alone his birthday and wedding anniversary.

Memory and recall are important, but it is knowledge that continues to astound me. Just think about all of the knowledge that is required for us to do even the most simplest of tasks with the modern day conveniences. What is even more astounding is that we can use that knowledge effectively and efficiently without having to understand it. We can carry this one step further. For the most part, not only do we lack the knowledge, we don't really care to have the knowledge and wouldn't know what to do with it if we did.

I like to equate this to an expert. Most of us have high regards for experts and we sort of accept them the same way I am impressed with those knowledgeable people on "Jeopardy". We know that they know something special. We also realize that not only do we not know what they know, but when they talk about what they know we don't have an inkling as to what they are talking about. For example, in my chosen field, I am considered an expert. But I have spent over 45 years learning about my field. Let me tell you about being an expert. When I was in 9th grade, my civics teacher, Mr. Bos, mentioned that every metallurgical engineer that graduated from the University of Michigan in 1954 had at least five job offers. Out of all the possible careers, I had already narrowed my selection down to being an engineer, but I didn't know what kind. So I looked up metallurgical engineering and decided to become one. I graduated and have two degrees. Then in the metallurgical field I narrowed it down even further and became interested in foundries. Still further, I narrowed it down to cast iron. Further still, I specialized in ductile cast iron and learned about such matters as inoculation and how to add 0.040% magnesium to iron to make it ductile. So, you see, based on what I have just told you, an expert is a person that knows every thing there is to know about practically nothing.

Most people don't even know that 0.040% magnesium is required to make iron ductile. In fact, most people don't even know that ductile iron is a special case cast iron. What's more, they don't even want to know and probably don't even care. We are all that way, aren't we. If it doesn't impact us why should we care?

Yet, to get along in this world, we must have some knowledge to exist. At least, we have come to some realization that our existence is dependent on some basic needs and we generally know how to fill those needs. We also know that potentially, God has provided for our most basic needs, all we have to do is use our God given talents to somehow fulfill those needs. A little horse trading shall we say? Some might say that although potentially the needs have been satisfied, perhaps the opportunity is sadly missing.

Our very existence is dependent on our knowledge of how to interact with our surroundings and with other people using our God given talents to gain some advantage so that we can exist. While we are at it, maybe we can exist without having to worry about having to continually interact to achieve that existence. We seek to find that easy road. We long to know what God is thinking so we can plan ahead and gain that elusive advantage to exist easier.

We continuously alter our concept of what God knows with the knowledge we gain from each moment of existence. Granted, our knowledge of creation is reinforced with repetitiveness. The big picture doesn't seem to change. Spring follows winter, summer follows spring, etc. However, we inherently seek opportunities to clarify our understanding of what God knows and how to interact with the rest of His creation. We constantly desire to interact without confrontation. We just plain want to have an uninterrupted path to our goal, whatever it is. We inherently want that path to be the right path. But we can't seem to see the path with the same knowledge that God has. For some reason, the path is paved with speed bumps and has curves we can not see around. Our image of God's will for our lives helps us make progress, but we constantly find ourselves in situations where God's direction is unclear.

We only have our experience in God's creation to relate to the greatness of God. Each of us has arrived at our current state of existence seeking an understanding of our creation that helps us to move to the next moment of existence. Our desire for an understanding of God usually is not the driving force for us to get to the next moment, yet, we acknowledge that our interaction with creation is a requirement for us to move on. We trust that creation will not come to an end before we realize our existence has moved on to the next moment.

A very close friend of mine believes "his god" knows the choice we are going to make before we make the choice. He says that if "his god" didn't know that much, then his god wasn't the god that he thought he was. Our personalization of God's knowledge is essential for us to develop some kind of understanding of how great God is. I think someone wrote a hymn by that name[5]. How great Thou art indeed! The greatness of God goes far beyond our imagination. It is great indeed that we can take a small part of what God knows and let that part be a guiding light for our existence.

Our knowledge of good and evil doesn't always seem to coincide with God's purpose for our lives. The choices we make are based on our limited knowledge of how those choices will interact with the rest of God's creation. All too often, the consequences of our decisions are not what we expected. Something was missing in our decision and we have difficulty understanding what that might be.

We blunder through the best we can and we pay the consequences. Some times, we wish that we had made a different choice because the consequences were so brutal. God's knowledge of His creation and our knowledge of His creation are definitely different. Why? Because we are convinced that the consequences in many instances were not the consequences we were expecting. Did God really "plan" it that way? I don't think so! But, did God know what was going to happen, Yes! On the other hand, maybe I am not giving God enough credit. Still, I am part of God's creation and His creation is much bigger than I can imagine. So, to assume that He didn't plan every step that I make is beyond the knowledge that He has given me.

"What evil lurks in the heart of man? The Shadow knows[6]" and so does God. Does He plan on you using it? Not no! but heck no. He plans on us using the good that lurks in our hearts not the evil. Yes, He knows that both exist there and yes He knows the consequences of our actions before we act, but does He know what action we are going to take before we act? If He did, then it would be impossible to make God angry. But the Bible is full of instances where God acted with vengeance because of the choices that his human creation made. God can become angry with our choices. He set out the rules. He gave us the ability to choose. He gave us an example of how to live, using Israel as the chosen people. And finally He came in person to show us how to live and how to make the right choices. Yet, we continually think we know more than He does and we continually try our way instead of His way. He expects us to act with His best interest at heart, not ours! Yet, isn't it strange that everything He asks of us is actually in our best interest. Israel was commanded to make animal sacrifices, but God ultimately said "do you think I need your sacrifices?"[1] "Do you think that if I were hungry I would tell you?"[2] Everything He asks of us is actually for us.

Easier said than done? With almost all of our circumstances, we do not always think, "God first". And more importantly, we do not always give God the glory!

How can we possibly think we know more than God? Maybe we don't know more than God, but I am not convinced that we always think that way. There certainly are times that we act like we think we know more than God. Why do we do that? What are we trying to get away with? What are we trying to prove? Do we think that by ignoring the existence of God we can manipulate our way into the limelight?

Are we so full of ourselves that we can possibly believe we can do God's work without God? Are we so omniscient that we think we can force God to alter His plan specifically for us? Are we so conceited that we believe God will accept our alternative without question? Are we so ignorant that we believe the knowledge we have is all that there is? Are we so arrogant that we think our thoughts are the only way to think? Are we so blind that we can't see that all inspiration comes from God? Are we so stupid that we believe our plan is better than God's plan?

Now, I think I have gone too far! What we think and what we know **IS** part of God's plan. What is even more important is that God's plan counts on us doing our part with the God given talents He has bestowed on us.

We may not know what God knows, but God knows what we know. Not only that, we know that God knows what we know. Interesting thought, isn't it? Yet, often times, we ignore the fact that God is aware of our every thought. We behave as if we are an island and that no bridges exist to our conscious self. Sometimes we behave as if all of our thoughts are original and that we are the only ones privy to what they are. Not only does God know what they are, it is surprising that others are seemingly able to read our minds. They may not have arrived at the same thought in the same way, but low and behold, they know what we are thinking or at least they think they do.

I am reminded of my children (and myself for that matter) telling me that they believed their mother and I had eyes in the back of our heads because of the many exploits they had secretly undertaken that we knew about. Their originality was only preceded by about 20 years of experience at having thought the same thing about our own parents. How silly we are to think that we alone have knowledge that we believe no one else has had. Granted, some of us do have original thoughts, otherwise, there would not be a need for an US Patent Office. Just the same, we are not as alone as we think we are. If we were, none of us would have a conscious.

We know the difference between right and wrong and we know that God knows the difference between right and wrong. What is more important is that we know that God knows we know the difference between right and wrong.

One of the movies that made a big impression on me when I was a teenager was "Rebel Without a Cause"[7] with James Dean. It was never explained to us whether the word "Rebel" was a noun or a verb. Being a rebel as a teenager seems to be the major way that most of us learn how to express our individuality. Also, most of us learn that being a rebel doesn't get us anywhere because we also learn that our parents are smarter than we thought they were. Isn't it amazing how intelligent our parents got while we were going from 13 years old to 18 years old? Somehow, we learned that rebelling without a cause was a useless endeavor. Nothing like taking the wind out of our "rebellious" sails before we even have a chance to see if our ideas would fly on their own. On the other hand we also learned that if we had a cause, most of the time our parents were willing to listen to us.

Our "rebellious" nature causes us to think that since we were created in God's image we can create too! And we can! The question is why do we think we can create without God? Just like our children, we rebel against authority just to show our independence. The Bible tells us that creating without God is creating in vain[3]. That's right! It is our vanity that causes us to think that we can create without God and thereby be as good as God. It is our vanity that causes us to think we are creators. It is our vanity that causes us not to give credit where the credit is due. We think that we know what is best for our lives. We think we know that what we are doing is what God wanted us to do. We go about our daily tasks simply believing that since we acknowledged that there is a God, we have done all that we need to do. We forget that all of our talents were created for us to be the individual that we are. We forget that we are working for His glory, not ours! His Glory! Lord, let your glory shine in us for all to see!

REFERENCE

1. Psalm 50:8
2. Psalm 50:12
3. Psalm 127:1
4. **Jeopardy!** is a syndicated American quiz show featuring trivia in topics such as history, literature, the arts, pop culture, science and sports. The show has a unique answer-and-question format in which contestants are presented with clues in the form of answers, and must phrase their responses in question form.
5. **"How Great Thou Art"** is a Christian hymn based on a Swedish poem written by Carl Gustav Boberg (1859–1940) in Sweden in 1885. The melody is a Swedish folk song. It was translated into English by British missionary Stuart K. Hine, who also added two original verses of his own composition.
6. **The Shadow** is a collection of serialized dramas, originally in pulp magazines, then on 1930s radio and then in a wide variety of media, that follow the exploits of the title character, a crime-fighting vigilante with psychic powers. One of the most famous pulp heroes of the 20th century, The Shadow has been featured in comic books, comic strips, television, video games, and at least five motion pictures. The radio drama is well-remembered for those episodes voiced by Orson Welles.
7. **Rebel Without a Cause** is a 1955 film directed by Nicholas Ray that tells the story of a rebellious teenager played by James Dean, who comes to a town, meets a girl, disobeys his parents, and defies the local high school bullies.

DISCUSSION QUESTIONS

1. Does GOD really know what we do before we do it?
2. Do you think GOD has a plan for you, or do you plan for GOD?
3. Is your knowledge self-attained, or part of GOD's gift to you?

THE KNOWLEDGE

CHAPTER 13

Why Isn't Having All Of This Knowledge Cracked Up To What It Is Supposed To Be?

Now that You have given us the freedom of choice,
There is no reason to seek Your voice! (YA RIGHT!)

Talk about a "time Out"! Consider the time out that God gave Adam and Eve when He threw them out of the Garden of Eden! This was a permanent "time out". His concern was that His man creatures might have learned more than He wanted them to learn. He didn't seem too concerned about their ability to exist in the wilderness. So, in His disgust, He "fed them to the wolves". He did give them clothes, however[1]. At that point, God was more than willing to let His human creation fend for themselves.

I can see it all now! At the risk of being criticized because of the liberties I am taking, let's turn this into a God-Man conversation.

God: "Adam, if you and Eve think you are so smart, get out of the garden and see what it is like in the wilderness where you will need to work very hard to sustain yourselves!"

Adam: "But God, how will we live? Where will we find food? How will we stay warm?"

God: "You should have thought about that before you decided to eat the forbidden fruit."

Adam: "But I didn't know you were going to throw us out."

God: "I warned you that you will surely die if you eat the forbidden fruit. You ought to be thankful that you are even alive, instead of worrying about how you will survive."

Adam: "But you have always provided for us in the past, how will we exist now?"

God: "I already told you! Work for it! I was willing to let you live on easy street, but no! You wanted to know what I knew. You listened to others tell you what was important. You wanted to make your own creation. You thought you could do it without me. You wanted to choose for yourselves. So, now you have that chance. I have given you all that you need to have, so get on with your existence. Just don't come back to the Garden of Eden."

Adam: "But God, there are so many things I don't know!"

God: "You should have thought about that before you took that bite! I am positive that you will learn as you go along. After all, I created you in my own image."

Adam: "That, somehow, doesn't reassure me! You know how all of these things work, but I don't".

God: "OK, I'll tell you what! You can have your choice in all matters between good and evil. Just remember, your choice now has consequences. You have just learned your first lesson on consequences. I hope that this is the worst consequence you will ever experience."

And so it begins.

The nature of this beginning caused me to stop and think of how those first days in the wilderness might have gone. God didn't seem to be concerned about Adam and Eve's ability to survive. Maybe because He was so down right disappointed with what they had done, He didn't really care. He knew the consequences, otherwise, He wouldn't have clothed them[1] and he also knew that they would have a hard row to hoe[2], so to speak. God seemed to be more concerned about issues other than whether or not His man creation would survive. God was fearful that man might live forever with this knowledge of good and evil[3]. Could it be that the corruption this knowledge would cause might spoil the perfection in His garden creation?

Mankind views this act a little differently than simply being thrown out of the Garden of Eden. We claim it was the beginning of having the freedom of choice. Actually they already had freedom of choice since they were freely following God's way. Perhaps, however, this was the beginning of humanity using that freedom in ways that were contrary to God! Somehow, whichever way it is considered, I believe freedom of choice was a long way from Adam and Eve's minds as they made their way into the wilderness during those first few days. Yet, having this new found freedom must have been exciting to them. On one hand they received the excitement they were seeking, but on the other hand they were given challenges that they had not expected. Freedom and hard work just seem to go together. Time for fun loving freedom does not come without working hard to provide the sustenance required for existence. Definitely, having knowledge of good and evil didn't crack up to being what they had imagined!

As we have learned since, freedom of choice comes with responsibilities. These responsibilities must be given our attention if we desire to maintain that freedom. We couldn't have the first amendment in our Constitution without also having some responsibility for applying those rights evenly and justly. We as individuals cannot abuse those freedoms or cause others to suffer because we have "the right" to those freedoms. If we do, freedoms are no longer freedoms.

Applying those freedoms equally and justly seems to be an argumentative issue that many claim isn't being accomplished fairly. Interesting claim, isn't it? Is it real? Or is the claim simply a way that others take advantage of the freedom to satisfy their own selfish nature. (Snake appears again and seems to have forced the freedom givers to cower in response.) God didn't cower! He threw Adam and Eve out of the Garden. Maybe we should take a lesson from God here and throw those snake following, selfish freedom using people, those people that are only looking out for themselves into the wilderness! Except, I don't know how to do that since all of us are already in the wilderness to begin with!

So, Adam and Eve were expecting great things to happen once they bit into the forbidden fruit. Great things happened, all right, but those "things" were not what Adam and Eve expected! Instead of becoming God like, they were exiled to the wilderness. Instead of living on easy street, they were required to fend for themselves and work for their livelihood. Instead of having God make all of the decisions, they had to decide for them-selves. And on top of it all, they had to learn how to make those decisions with the knowledge of good and evil lurking in the back of their minds. This wasn't at all what they expected!

So much for expectations! Adam and Eve didn't know they had it so good until it was taken away from them. Once they were on their own, reality set in and God took on a different role. Reality became the difference between expectations and experience. As an engineer, that is an interesting equation:

$$\text{Expectations} - \text{Experience} = \text{Reality!}$$

Existence became a bundle of disappointments. God became even more disappointed with His human creation when they failed to use their new freedom without "experiencing" even more selfish trouble. Mankind was disappointed that knowing what God knew about good and evil didn't make them like God. Not only was the human creature disappointed about not becoming like God, humans found that they didn't know how to exist without God. They found that the presence of God in their lives was necessary to counteract the evil part of good and evil. They found that sorting the difference between good and evil required even more knowledge, and that they had to acquire it. They also found that they needed to think for themselves and that they needed the wisdom of God to accomplish the sorting tasks.

Humans found that thinking for themselves without involving God, and without thinking about the rest of God's creation had consequences. These consequences exceeded their capacity to understand. These lessons go on and on. Even more important, these lessons require humans to relearn them with every generation. In fact, we often find that the relearning doesn't require waiting for the next generation. All too often humans find themselves in the same predicament over and over and over again. We never seem to learn that living in the wilderness with the freedom of choice isn't enough to sustain our existence. Where is God when we really need Him?

Even when we know the difference, knowledge of good and evil isn't enough. Making the correct choice seems to have so many different consequences that we can't possibly reconcile them all. We can't say that God didn't warn us! Instead of the rewards Adam and Eve were expecting, they found a complex, intertwined matrix of understanding that compounds itself beyond imagination.

Instead of becoming even closer to God, they were pushed into the wilderness. Instead of knowing what God knew, they found their knowledge was limited. Instead of being equal to God living freely, they found that they had to use God's creation to eek out a meager existence. Instead of gaining an advantage, they lost all of the advantages they had.

Life in the wilderness definitely wasn't what Adam and Eve were expecting when they took that bite. What happened anyway? All of the glorious things they had imagined did not turn out as they expected. The new knowledge they gained did not make life what they thought it would be. Life was not cracked up to be what they thought it should be. They could blame it on Snake if they wanted, but you and I both know that the existence they received was the consequence of their actions. These consequences were the price for _their_ actions, not the actions of others. The shackles that go along with the freedom of choice required them to think for themselves. The shackles required them to work for a living. The shackles required them to consider evil whenever they needed to make a decision for good. What a revelation! Man's way or God's way? And what is God's way any way? And then, AND THEN, they had to suffer the consequences!

Having that knowledge about the difference between good and evil definitely didn't do Adam and Eve any favors. It definitely didn't make their life any easier. Choices; too many choices. Consequences; too many consequences. How do we sort them all out? Sorting isn't easy. Too many issues to consider! Is there any way to go backwards and be allowed back into the Garden of Eden? Is there any way to get back into God's good graces?

Do we just try to get along or do we take a stand for what we think is right? Do we have enough knowledge to act or do we put it off until we know more? Do we know what is going to happen or do we think we know what is going to happen? How come if there is a 50/50 chance that a choice will be screwed up, 9 times out of 10 the choice is screwed up?

Evil exists in places Adam and Eve never imagined. Evil isn't like sound. Evil happens even when no one is there to experience it. You make a choice that you think is right and up pops evil just like it was waiting in that dark corner for you to make a mistake; a mistake that wasn't considered when you made your choice. Evil has its way of showing up subconsciously when we were hoping that we could get around it and sneak one of our choices into the system undetected. Evil and good don't go hand in hand. We think they do, because we are constantly paying the consequences. At least we think that we are always paying the consequences. Maybe our mind set is that we see more of the evil than the good because evil makes such a mess of things.

As I suggested earlier, evil is evil and there is no such thing as just a little evil. Fortunately, good is good and that is the way it is supposed to be. Good isn't looking for recognition! Fortunately as well, God **IS** looking for recognition! God threw Adam and Eve into the wilderness hoping to knock some sense into them. He gave them the freedom of choice so that they would come closer to Him. He was expecting results from His actions just like Adam and Eve were expecting consequences from taking that first bite of the forbidden fruit.

God's expectations are often disregarded. In fact, it probably rarely occurs to us that God has expectations. How could He have expectations? After all, He is the creator, isn't He? In our minds, everything in His creation is set in granite so why would He have expectations? Everything is so planned that nothing is left to chance in God's creation or at least that is how most of us think most of the time. Aren't all of God's expectations in fact instant realities? After all, God is the creator, and His name is "I AM"! Shouldn't His expectations simply just BE!

If God gave us freedom of choice, what was He expecting? In God's creation, where does freedom of choice fit in? God loves His creation. The life He has given us is for His glory. The talents He has given us are for His glory. The freedoms He has given us are for His glory. So what are His expectations? I believe the answer is HIS GLORY! Living up to God's expectations instead of our own may make life in the wilderness a little more rewarding. After all is said and done, He IS the creator!

REFERENCES

1. Genesis 3:21
2. Genesis 3:17-19
3. Genesis 3:22

DISCUSSION QUESTIONS

1. Do knowledge and freedom of choice go hand-in-hand?
2. Why do all our choices have consequences?
3. 'What does GOD expect of us?

THE KNOWLEDGE

CHAPTER 14

Does All This Knowledge of Good and Evil Make Us Think We Are God?

Good v. Evil is a contest to win;
Without God on our side, our chances are thin.

If God thinks we wouldn't like to be god then God should be rethinking creation! Not one of us can honestly say that we haven't at least thought about being lord over our own little world at one time or another. It may have been just a subtle thought about wanting something to happen the way we planned it; or the "thought" may be more than subtle and has engulfed our entire life's ambition. We want to be lord over our existence. We want to be lord over our universe. We rationalize. We justify. We use. We believe more in ourselves than we believe in others. And God, why would we consider God? After all, we were the one that managed to finagle the circumstances, not God. Most of us don't even think about God, let alone consider God, as the driving force for our little universe. We leave God out until we get into trouble. Then, we think, oh yah, God, please help. Then after He doesn't help we get angry that HE isn't fixing it just the way we want. Golly, He has the power doesn't He? We expect God to serve our desires, but give little thought to His.

We would only be fooling ourselves if each one of us didn't admit that we want to be in charge of our own destiny. Our mind and our thoughts drive us to be the best we can be. We tell ourselves that we are willing to learn, but we work very hard to keep the minds and thoughts of others from changing our direction. In that sense, we are as independent as a hog on ice. We believe no one can take care of us better than we can take care of ourselves, no matter what. We have a hard time believing that others can influence or control our minds. What a dichotomy! We want to learn, but we don't want anybody telling us what to do. We want more knowledge, but we don't want anybody to know what we don't know. On the other hand, these "don't wants" conflict with the fact that having a friend to learn with is exciting.

If God hadn't given us the ability to reason, life would be so much simpler. We wouldn't have to rationalize; we wouldn't have to justify; we wouldn't have to connive; we would just try to make our own way. Just a little food and shelter would be all that we need. But no, what do we do? A little evil here, a little evil there, what could it hurt? As I suggested earlier, there is no such thing as a little evil. Why can't we set our minds to think GOOD?

It isn't difficult to pretend that we know more than we actually know. After all, we can't appear stupid in front of our friends. It isn't difficult to lead others to think we know what we are doing. They are too busy with their own facades.

The difficulty is admitting that we are running our lives by the seat of our pants. The difficulty is that we don't always understand the consequences of our actions. The difficulty is knowing when we have offended someone. The difficulty is the same as Adam and Eve, understanding good and evil in every situation. The difficulty is accepting that God and His creation come first. The difficulty is accepting that we can not make anything that God has not already created. The difficulty is that our originality has another origin. We forgot that God created it in the first place. All we did was discover what already existed.

We tell ourselves that defining our roles in God's creation is definitely dependent on **our** thinking and no one else's. However, as we grow older and wiser, we learn that identifying our role in God's creation is more than a simple challenge. Hell, defining our roles in our own creation is more than a simple challenge.

My wife and I have been married for over 48 years (to each other). As I look back over those years, defining our roles with respect to each other was always the challenge. We made this agreement early in our relationship: before we were married, we agreed that she would be boss; after we were married, we agreed I would be boss, but she would get her own way. It has worked brilliantly. In fact after gathering all of this knowledge of good and evil for the last 45 years, I have to say we made a very wise choice. Evil has crept in many times, but we have always managed to sidestep the major potholes that could have been a result. I am not saying that our marriage is perfect and without blemishes; what I am saying is that we always (so far) have managed to work the issues out to minimize the damage in our relationship. In fact, our relationship has become stronger as a consequence of working out our differences. Love does wonderful things! Respect is even more rewarding.

Our roles in our own little universe are always changing. Some times we need to reinforce others and sometimes others need to reinforce us. So we do the same as Adam and Eve, we try to become god of our existence. We fall prey to our own desires. We forget that God was the real creator. We forget that at one time we didn't have knowledge of good and evil. In fact, I would venture to say that we forget that we have knowledge of good and evil all together. When we come right down to it, we forget where knowledge of any kind began in the first place.

Knowledge begins with respect for the Lord[1]. That was the ultimate lesson when God kicked Adam and Eve out of the Garden; respect. If Adam and Eve had respected God's request in the first place, they wouldn't have needed the knowledge of good and evil. They wouldn't have needed a freedom of choice. They could have lived forever in the lap of luxury!

Such was not the case! Adam and Eve failed to respect God's request. They wanted to "be like God". They abused the privileges that God had given them and God found that He needed to teach them respect. In so doing, freedom of choosing a way that was not God's way was born. Now, consequences would result from their actions. Now, good and evil would be ever entwined in every choice. Now, knowledge of good and evil would have to be respected. Now, God would get the respect He deserved. Now God would be able to work out the differences. Now man might be able to understand who is boss. Now, disappointment would abound! If, we don't think that disappointment abounds, just think back to the last time you disappointed God. Didn't have to think back very far did you!

Creation was about to experience mankind with all of their selfish nature. Creation was about to experience an influence that was not God. Creation was about to experience a creature that wanted to be a god and didn't know how. Knowledge begins with respect for the Lord. God was about to experience a creature that had to learn respect. God was about to experience a stubborn, self-centered, know-it-all, blowhard who needed to learn how to use knowledge; who needed to learn how to respect knowledge. Was God expecting this? Remember:

Expectation – Experience = Reality (Even for God, I think)

It isn't a matter of knowledge any longer; it is a matter of respect. Knowledge alone isn't enough. Knowledge of good and evil was just the beginning. We can't possibly know as much as God. No one among us has enough knowledge to make something out of nothing like God did. Knowledge of good and evil is nothing compared to the knowledge required to create the universe. Yet, we act like the ability to choose between good and evil is the only requirement to be the "go to person" in our own little universe.

The smallness of our minds needs to wake up to the vastness of God. All we have to do is look around. If the result of God's creation isn't obvious, think about the simple things. Think about the things that mankind has made with God's creation that completely confound us. We don't know anything by comparison.

We can't possibly think that we can even come close to being comparable to God. Yet, we do. We constantly disregard how we managed to get where we are. Maybe we need another "big bang" to wake us up to the fact that creation didn't just happen.

The first story of creation in the Bible tells us that God created light[2], and that was good[3]! No evil existed in that creation. Then God created Heaven[4]. No evil existed in that creation. God then created Earth and that was good[5]. Next, God created the stars and the moon[6], and that was good[7]. No evil in that creation. Creatures of the sea and birds were next[8], and that was good. No evil there either. Land creatures were next[9], and that was good as well. Then God made man[10]. After that, God declared his creation very good[11]. No evil existed up until that time.

Once man started creating, the size of the universe became relatively small. Once mankind began abusing freedom of choice, evil took root. Man can't possibly know as much as God, because evil gets in the way. "Good" is still there, but we had to learn how to sort out the difference. It seems that somehow mankind has mucked up creation for one simple reason — we desire to be the determining factor in what is good and what is evil for our own little creations. Who can blame us? After all, we were created in God's image. Disappointment indeed abounds! We become disappointed that our creations don't perform all of the tasks that we think they should. We become disappointed that others don't revere our creations with the same awe that we do. We become disappointed that no one seems to be patting us on the back for doing such a good job. So what does God expect us to do? If we aren't smart enough to be god of our own little universe, what does God expect of us?

We keep learning that our choices have consequences. We keep learning that what we expect to happen as the result of our choices is not always the way it happens. "Expectations versus reality" is a contest. How do we gain the wisdom to always know the outcome? Where do we go to find the information that we are expected to have so that we can always make the correct choice? Where does the information exist that helps us understand our impact on God's "Good" creation? How do we gain the knowledge that God wants us to have to make the right choice every time? I don't know! But I do know this: God hasn't given up on us yet!

He has tried at least three times to show us how He wants us to live in His universe. Adam and Eve was His first try. He gave them the freedom of choice! That didn't work. Then He chose a people. The result was nearly just as bad! The Israelites time and again refused to honor His choice of direction and they suffered the consequences. Yet, there were sparks of righteousness in the ranks of the Israelites over the centuries. The Bible is full of wonderful examples. The Bible is also full of consequences from bad choices. Have we learned yet? Not on your life. No wonder God had to come in person to show us how to honor His creation. Have we learned yet?

REFERENCES

1. Proverbs 1:7
2. Genesis 1:3
3. Genesis 1:4
4. Genesis 1:7
5. Genesis 1:10
6. Genesis 1:16
7. Genesis 1:18
8. Genesis 1:21
9. Genesis 1:25
10. Genesis 1:27
11. Genesis 1:31

DISCUSSION QUESTIONS

1. Do you ever ask for GOD's help or guidance when you are not in trouble?
2. In spite of all our human failures, do you think GOD has given up on us?
3. Do you respect what GOD has given you?

THE CONSEQUENCES

CHAPTER 15

Now That You Are On Your Own, What Are You Going To Do?

When we leave home to be on our own
Our minds think we are doing it alone.

Independence, there is nothing like independence. We can't wait to get out from under that ruling thumb. I will never forget the first time the boss told me to go ahead with an original idea I had. I was so scared! Although I had been working for over eight years in my chosen profession, I was flabbergasted that the boss had accepted something I had recommended without telling me what a hair-brained idea it was. He didn't pick the idea apart; he didn't restructure the idea; and he didn't claim any of the "recognition and glory" as his. Fortunately, that first experience was a success and in fact set the standard for similar occasions and has not been surpassed in over 30 years.

We don't always have that type of successful consequence. However, when it happens, it is exhilarating to be able to put your thumbs in your suspenders and puff out your chest. We can look back at those experiences and judge them to be "Good". While they are in their planning stages though, our heart sank with the knowledge that we have put our ego on the line. Once we stop procrastinating and make the commitment, we have no choice except to follow through and do the best we can to make certain that we don't falter. We don't know where the pitfalls are. We don't know where the help we need is gong to come from. We don't know where the "snake pits" are (how the devil will intervene). It is amazing to me how quickly we learn; how ready we are with advice for the next time the task is attempted; and how expert we become with the task.

Adam and Eve certainly didn't know where the pitfalls were going to be. Were they scared? I would say, "You bet your bipy they were scared!" Was this what they wanted? I don't know. But, I do know that they were warned. My best guess is that they wanted their independence or at least what they envisioned would be their independence. My guess is also that what they envisioned was not what they received. God said, "So, you want your independence eh! OK! Here it is and here are the conditions that go along with you receiving your independence."

They didn't leave empty handed. The last thing that God did before He threw Adam and Eve out of the Garden was dress them.[1] Just before that, however, God made it clear that they understood the consequences. Women owe it to Eve for the pain they suffer during child birth[2] and men owe it to Adam for having to work for a living[3]. (I think that women received a double dose, especially those women that want both children and a career since they also have to work for a living if they want to show men how to do it.)

Consequences, these are truly consequences, but they hadn't experienced the biggest consequence of them all, returning to dust[4]! "Luckily", I suppose, they would only experience it once. Adding it all up, considering all of the ramifications, Adam and Eve gave up eternal life in their quest for knowledge of good and evil. They couldn't say the God didn't warn them. God told them unequivocally exactly what would happen[5]! Of course, maybe, since they were the first, one has to ask did death have a meaning?

In any event, Adam and Eve were told the consequences, yet they went ahead and did their apple eating deed anyway. Their goal was to know as much as God. They couldn't really anticipate the consequences. What did they know about death? What did they know about hard work? For that matter, what did they know about work at all? What did they know about having children? They were about to experience a reality that would for ever be between them and God, and that reality still wouldn't allow them to know as much as God knew.

I look back at my example where I was told to go ahead with my idea. I had no knowledge about how to put my idea together. Adam and Eve had no knowledge about how to grow food. They had no experience with keeping themselves protected from the elements. I had no expectations if the idea didn't work. As with Adam and Eve, ignorance is bliss. As I look back at my experience, I was truly blessed with a great idea and with some great experience resource. My employer had knowledge that I didn't have and they had confidence in my idea. Most of all, they had confidence in me. I believe that all of these factors existed for Adam and Eve as well. God knew that his man creation had it within their ability to conquer existing in the rest of His creation. Adam and Eve had a great resource as well. The question is, would they learn how to use it? As with my employer and my idea, God would not let them fail. They might have to learn a few hard lessons just as I did with my unique idea mentioned above. Even though my boss gave me the go ahead without interfering or claiming any credit for the project, he was not about to let me fail and neither was God about to let Adam and Eve fail. No matter, consequences still existed. We usually do not have any idea what all of the consequences will be when we set out to fulfill <u>our</u> desires, and that is a problem.

If we always knew what all of the consequences would be would we still set out to take on our deeds? Good question. Do we think that if Adam and Eve knew what death was like, or what hard work meant, or how painful childbirth would be, they wouldn't have defied God? Another good question!

So what is the answer? I believe that human creation with their entire God given curiosity would have always done what Adam and Eve did. We can't help ourselves. We must, by our very nature, step into the unknown with blind curiosity. We must learn for ourselves that God's way involves experiencing great frustration with our inability to do it all by ourselves. We must experience the unexpected to appreciate the wisdom that is available to us if we only look a little harder. We must find where the fences are so that we can live within our limitations. Unfortunately, most of us do not believe the limitations when we find them. Then again, maybe it isn't unfortunate. Maybe the risk of crossing the fence is worth it. Maybe, the fence was our imagination in the first place.

Looking at today's people, I can see this natural curiosity. However, I can also see considerable reluctance. Is the reluctance natural? I don't think so! I think the reluctance is the direct result of Adam and Eve's experience. Their consequences were harsh enough that some people do not want to challenge the possibilities and simply DO NOT step out. That doesn't mean that they don't have the curiosity, it means that they don't want the imagined consequences. Which is right? I don't know! For me, however, I like the challenges; and the things I learn; and the opportunities I experience. Life can be exciting when put in the proper perspective!

When God's man creation parted company with God, man had to learn many hard lessons. In fact, humans are still learning those lessons. The consequences of those lessons reoccur all of the time. One would think that humans should be able to pass on the consequences of those lessons. My children will tell you otherwise. Try as we might, we parents become very frustrated trying to keep our children from experiencing bad consequences from their actions. No easy way exists for any of us to pass on these lessons without some rebellion and in some cases a lot of rebellion.

Basically, my wife and I have concluded that two ways exist to raise children. Both ways involve tremendous amounts of love and caring concern. One way is to allow the children to experience controlled independence with a gradual release of the unseen security blanket. The second way is to provide a security net for every action. The first way leads to total independence and children that are quite capable of living on their own. The second way leads to continued dependence and children that are always around home. Both choices have their good sides and their bad sides. At the extreme, the first way will lead to having children that you never see because they are so independent; the second way has children you see all of the time, but they don't know how to live without you (or your provisions). Finding that happy middle ground is difficult! However, my wife and I have found the solution! Grandchildren! My wife agrees that if we knew what caused grandchildren, we might have done more about it. Grandchildren permit you to spoil them rotten and then hand them back to the parents to deal with in the real world. Our children don't understand, yet!

I am not about to guess what God was thinking when He made the rules about the tree of knowledge of good and evil. Nor am I about to guess what God was thinking when He threw Adam and Eve into the wilderness. I can only offer some opinions based on the experiences that God has allowed me to have in His creation. When that initial separation between humans and God occurred, it wasn't only mankind that had to pay the consequences; God experienced consequences as well. We generally only think about the consequences to humans. After all we can best relate to the human part in this story. We can understand the disappointment humans had when the consequences of their actions were not even part of their vision or experience in the first place. Humans couldn't be intimidated by visualizing something they had never seen or experienced.

It is very difficult to relate to God's part in this story. Giving humans their independence meant that the relationship He was expecting would be more difficult to develop. As mankind set out on their own, they would soon learn that good consequences resulted from their actions as well as bad consequences. Humans would learn that both pleasure and disappointment could be experienced with God's creation. Humans would also learn that they had some measure of control over experiencing the good consequences and the pleasures. As these good consequences and pleasures occurred, mankind started to maneuver their experiences so that these good consequences and pleasures would occur on demand or so they thought. If you always do what you have always done, you will always get what you always got so to speak.

As these good consequences and pleasures mounted, repetition of the pleasure was sought. It is easy to understand how the desire for the pleasant experience would result in a desire for repetition of the experience. It is also easy to understand how some of these experiences might be associated with some unrelated creation or experience. For example, this association might be similar to a man who plays baseball not changing his underwear or not shaving during a winning streak. Instead of giving God credit for His creation, humans begin to think that their good consequences and pleasures occur because of some creation that they made, rather than God. As a result, idols were born and worship of man-made creations began.

The Bible teaches us that we don't have to go very far before these good consequences and pleasures have a negative effect. In fact, dire consequences of the second order resulted in the very next generation after Adam and Eve. Cain, their first born son, killed his brother, the second born son, because Able had a pleasure that Cain didn't have[6].

God's disappointment didn't end with throwing Adam and Eve out of the Garden. Humans have continued to disappoint God with nearly everything they do. The right relationship just didn't seem to develop between man and God, no matter what God did. The consequences were that humans don't appreciate God's creation and the relationship God was expecting was lost in mankind's "creations".

Yes, there is nothing like independence. It is a wonderful thing. However, independence can cause a certain amount of pride of accomplishment. This pride inhibits recognizing that the independence was, in fact, intentional and had nothing to do with the receiver. The entire act of independence was deliberate and intentional. It was not a random act of kindness. It was an act designed to bring man closer to God. It was an act designed to teach us that we needed God. It was an act that God deliberately took to have us be thankful for

His creation. God continues to expect us to be dependent on Him in our independence. Acknowledging God's creation and showing appreciation in return is the least we can do.

REFERENCES

1. Genesis 3:21
2. Genesis 3:16
3. Genesis 3:17
4. Genesis 3:19
5. Genesis 2:17
6. Genesis 4:8

DISCUSSION QUESTIONS

1. When you are good, are you really good? Does it matter?
2. GOD's first threat to Adam and Eve did not work! Do threats work in your life today?
3. What have you learned from your most recent failure?

THE CONSEQUENCES

CHAPTER 16

What's Up With Your Neighbor?
Having Trouble Keeping Up With The Joneses?

The driving force in our life
Improperly directed can lead to strife.

I belong to a sharing group that has used study books by Max Lucado, Joel Osteen, Rick Warren, John Eldredge, Bill Huebsch, and several others. On more than a few occasions during the course of discussing the contents of these books, the subject of the "stuff" we own has been the topic of conversation. I remember one particular discussion when quite a few members voiced their desire not to live without all of their stuff, me included. I don't know about you folks, but my world is full of "stuff". Isn't it amazing what we collect over the years?

We recently moved from a home where we resided for nine years. I can't tell you how many trips I made to Goodwill. Not only that, the trips I made were to give away boxes full of "stuff" that had not been opened from the move made nine years previously as well as new "stuff" we had collected. We had lived in our previous home for more than twenty-five years. So you can imagine the magnitude of the "stuff" that we had collected. In fact, I didn't want to move because I knew the task required cleaning out my garage.

I had coffee cans full of nuts and bolts. They were collected over the years just so that I wouldn't have to make another trip to the hardware store to buy what I needed to repair some item that had broken. What did I do? I went to the hardware store anyway.

Recently, however, we have moved to a remote location in the middle of the Manistee National Forrest in Michigan. A round trip to town is 50 miles. Needless to say, I have learned to look in my coffee cans before I go traipsing off to the hardware store.

Do we amass such useless resources just because we can or for our convenience or because we are competing with some imagined foe? The answer is, "YES" (probably to both and to much more). We are so spoiled with the ease to accumulate man made things; we forget that these "things" are the consequence of learning how to exist after being thrown into the wilderness. We treat this accumulation as if it is a badge of accomplishment, and maybe it is. More likely it is a display of privilege, or false need, or opportunity, or some other man made excuse.

I think that if we look back to the original event where Adam and Eve were "dismissed" from the Garden, maybe all of this stuff is the result of circumstances and the desire to survive no matter what. Perhaps, however, we have gone beyond the desire to survive and are enjoying nothing more than self indulgence. If we think about the original Garden of Eden, I can't help but believe that we have exaggerated the basic needs for existence. On the other hand, maybe the cartoonic exhibit of what the original Garden of Eden was like is an exaggeration of reality in the first place. I also can't help but think that we have digressed considerably from existence in the Garden of Eden. The difference is dependence or perhaps conceived dependence. In the Garden we were totally dependent on God for subsistence. In the wilderness, our conception was that we were dependent on our own abilities even though these abilities were given to us by God. Independence, as we discovered in the last chapter, is a wonderful thing. But, independence can lead to falsely believing we are capable of sustaining ourselves.

I don't want to introduce the notion that accumulating wealth is a reward from God for our steadfast devotion at this point, but who are we trying to impress? I submit to you that God is not impressed with anything that can be labeled "stuff". It is all temporary. The difference between accumulating stuff for self indulgence and impressing God is so vast that I don't believe we are capable of completely understanding the significance of the difference without divine intervention.

I believe that God wants us to have the best. However, there may be a gap between what God thinks is the best and what mankind thinks is the best. The way that mankind judges what is best and the way that God judges what is best introduces different driving forces; the difference is between what is seen and what is unseen. The difference is between material "stuff" and spiritual "stuff". The difference is between what we know and what we don't know. The difference is between what we can feel and touch and what we believe we can accomplish. The difference is between faith in what mankind can do and faith in what God can do.

Have you watched the game show "Deal or No Deal"[1]? Contestants say they believe that the $1,000,000.00 is in the case they have chosen. So far I have only seen the $1,000,000.00 in the chosen case once. The reality is that all of the rest of the time some other amount is in the chosen case. The real reality is that the only real money is the offer the banker makes for the chosen case.

In many instances, the same "deal" exists for us. We have a hard time believing that the real thing isn't the offer, but rather the "stuff that is in our case" is reality. You can't blame us? We have worked very hard for the stuff in our case. We can see it, we can feel it, we can use it, and we can call it our own. In fact, many times, we even have a title that says we own it. But, it is all temporary. Nothing lasts forever, or does it?

One of the consequences of being thrown out of the Garden of Eden is that mankind developed a false sense of accomplishment. To say that God was disappointed is an understatement. But to say that God didn't care is a gross misjudgment. God's love for his creation has no bounds. The only bounds are "fences" that mankind has made. The "stuff" that we have might be part of those fences, but that "stuff" might be the result of God wanting us to have the best.

As I think about history, I can't help but look at the progress and advancement that mankind has made in understanding and using God's creation. For example, out of all history, it has only been in the last two hundred fifty years that mankind has been able to travel with locomotion that goes beyond foot power. Steam power and the internal combustion engine have made it possible to experience God's creation in an abundant way. Yet, as a consequence of this freedom, mankind has managed to surrender his independence and has become a slave to desires to out do one another. We can't help but want better things than we had a moment ago or worse, better things than our brother or our neighbor.

I have two brothers that are close in age to each other and a lot younger than I am. They truly enjoy each other's company and do things together constantly. Their names are so close to each other that some people don't know who is who. In fact, I have heard them referred to in tandem as if they were one person. Their names are Tom and Tim. On the outside looking in, it has always appeared to me that whatever one has the other one will get. They don't really try to out do each other but, they don't let the other get ahead either. I will admit, however, they have a lot of fun. Their choice of beverage is the same. Their choice of motorcycle ride is the same. Their choice of drive is the same. Sometimes they include me. In some issues, I try to emulate them. But in many instances, I would rather go my own way. Although together they demonstrate many likenesses, when they are apart, they have definite identities. Others try to emulate certain aspect of their togetherness. One of the most outstanding attributes that they have is love: love for each other; love for life; and love for others.

Keeping up with my brothers isn't a bad thing unless the only thing you want to emulate is the rides and the drinks and some of the other "stuff". They don't really care if you keep up or not. However, you are always invited to join them and if you do, I guarantee you will have fun; tubing down the river; playing cards; throwing horse shoes; eating fish at their fish fry; eating pig at their corn roast; riding your motorcycle to the blessing of the bikes; camping; or just sitting around having a drink or two (or three). Sharing what they have is their fun. We all share, but most of the time we only share what we want to share and hold back many of the possibilities that we could share.

One of the consequences of being dismissed from the Garden or being thrown into the wilderness or what ever you want to call it is learning how to share. Over the millenniums, sharing was necessary to survive. Not everyone could successfully farm although they tried. Not everyone could do the tasks necessary to exist, although they tried. Ultimately, the existence tasks became divided. Some farmed, some gathered, some made clothing, some made shelters, but they all shared. I tell my wife that if I lived in earlier eras, I probably would have been a blacksmith instead of a metallurgical engineer. We even developed a means to trade our sharing. It is called money.

Sharing, however, has lead to other human attributes. Some of these attributes have their good side and some have their bad sides. One thing for certain, all of us like to have control over the sharing we do. We want the sharing to be our idea if we are going to share. Being expected to share is not good. Being forced to share is even worse. Being told to share is not good. Being told, "I owe it to someone to share" is even worse.

Ayn Rand in her book "Atlas Shrugged" (ref. pg 76 #2) shows what can happen when mankind is required to share depending on need. When we are told what we must share and when we must share it without our input, our tendency is to rebel against the authority. The book also reveals what happens from the "receiving" side as well. For some reason, we develop a false need so that we get "our fair share". The ultimate consequence is that man's creativity is withheld because we don't like being used without our consent.

In pure utopia, we are all "used". In pure utopia, we all need each other. In pure utopia, we give because we can. In pure utopia, we don't receive unless we need. In pure utopia, we don't hoard. In pure utopia, our God given talents are of equal value. In pure utopia, everyone strives to be their best. In pure utopia, everyone considers everyone else as equal. In pure utopia, there is no richer or poorer. We all share. We all are dependent on each other. Pure utopia is redundant, since utopia by definition is pure!

Such is not the case. Utopia only exists in our minds. We put a value on the talent that we share. We put value on being prepared. We put value on the time we play and the playthings we have. We put value on the friends we have because of the things they have. We decide who we are going to share with and we decide what we are going to share. Except, of course, for the taxes we pay. Even then we vote for the persons we think will tax the way we want. In the end, taxes make us all victims of equal opportunity.

Just think of all the things that this sharing business has led to. Because some people think that sharing doesn't require permission, we have invented more stuff like locks. We have words like mine and security. We have regulations like speed laws and stop signs. We have people who determine how much we share and we have "civilization" full of people that are givers, takers, and "wanters".

God wanted humanity to suffer the consequence of disobedience and we have!

REFERENCES

1. "Deal or No Deal" was (or is) an NBC television show from 2008- 2010 where 26 brief cases (one for each letter of the alphabet) contained unknown but designated amounts of cash up to $1,000,000.00. A contestant chose one case at the start of the contest and was offered various amounts of cash to sell his case after opening various other brief cases. The amount being offered for the chosen case depended on what cases had been opened. Obviously, if the $1,000,000.00 remained unopened the offers for the case the contestant chose went up accordingly. The contestant really didn't know how much was in his case until the end of the contest when he either sold it for the amount being offered or he retained it.

DISCUSSION QUESTIONS

1. What stuff in your life is really important?
2. How would life be if you were not so needy, or greedy?
3. Are you sharing your talents without expecting a return?

THE CONSEQUENCES

CHAPTER 17

Which Way Do I Go? Is My G.P.S. Working?

No matter which way I look, everything is the same
But to the directionally unimpaired, this excuse is lame.

When I was a young teenager, deer hunting with my step father and step uncles and step cousins was a blast. My cousins, my brother, and I were not old enough to carry guns, but what a great time we had being out with the grownups. Some of the lessons we learned are not allowed to be repeated (the grownups had swear words that I didn't know they knew), but despite that restriction some tales manage to be told anyway. Since we were energetic kids and didn't carry guns, we did the driving and the grownups did the shooting. By driving, I mean we were the ones that walked through the woods to drive out the deer. You might think that driving out the deer was just a stroll through the woods. However, this stroll was way more than you are thinking. We drove whole sections of land and sometimes more. For those of you who are not familiar with this country term, a "section" of land is a mile square. Each of us kids had to walk through that section driving the deer to the grownups standing or sitting at the sides and at the end of the section. This arrangement allowed the adults to have an opportunity to complete their hunt. (That is a polite way of saying to harvest a deer.)

Our walk through the woods was always interesting. We were placed along a line and given some kind of signal to start our walk so that we were in unison. Usually at least one grown-up came along with us kids. (But, they cheated. It wasn't always the same grown up and we might do four or five of these drives a day. The kids were always drivers!) The signal consisted of some agreed to time interval that was required for the setters to get into position. Once we started the drive and were in the woods, we couldn't see the next guy in line on either side. Sometimes we hollered and yelled, but when we were underway, the drive required concentration so that we didn't stray off course. This concentration was needed since we were in the woods with no point of reference going up and down hills and around trees or swamps. We kids were given a compass and were always provided a compass heading. We were also provided with instructions about when to end the drive. These instructions were "when you get to a road" or "when you come to a two track" or "when get to a fence line" or some other recognizable land mark; stop and wait for a grownup to come and get you. Once we got to the end, we would all wait until someone came. We would then walk to some convenient location so that we could be picked up and hauled to the next spot or go and retrieve the animal harvest.

I remember one drive in particular. My brother, Mike, was at the far right with all the rest of the drivers on his left and none on his right. We were all told to stop when we got to a fence line. All of us drivers completed the mile long drive to a north south fence line. As we stood around recounting the deer that we had seen, and how many of the sitters had missed their targets, and how many deer were down, some one said, "Where's Mike?"

Sure enough, Mike was not with us and was not where he was supposed to be. We waited and waited and waited. Finally my uncle Bob declared that he would walk back through the woods taking the path that Mike should have taken but in reverse. Uncle Bob seemed to know where every thing was and usually didn't need a compass. The rest of us went back to the place where we began the drive and waited as Uncle Bob walked through the woods looking for Mike.

Uncle Bob found Mike about half way between the start and finish. They came walking out of the woods with Uncle Bob in the lead. Everyone was elated that nothing had happened to Mike. He was safe and sound and was not lost after all. Mike had explicitly followed the directions he had been given before we started. When he got to a fence, he stopped. It must have been pretty lonely. He had waited and waited just like we did. But nobody came. We were accustomed to all gathering around after the drive just talking about what we saw and where we would be going next. But for Mike, that wasn't happening this time. He was standing all alone waiting at the fence line like he was told. Fortunately, he had stayed put and didn't wander off. The misunderstanding was the fence. We were supposed to walk to a north-south fence line and Mike, being on the far right, didn't know that the right side of the woods had a fence line that ran east-west. Being on the outside of the drive line, he had wandered a little off course and encountered that east-west fence line. He stopped just like he was told. Good thing too! It is hard to say what would have happened if he had crossed the fence even though it was the wrong fence. We would probably still be looking for him.

Other aspects of life can be related to this "off course" experience that Brother Mike had. Take my career for example. I have enjoyed finding the fences. However, the consequences are that I usually managed to cause the bosses some consternation. They would rather that I didn't push the boundaries, which is what I usually did (and still do as a matter of fact). Once I found the fence, I couldn't help myself. My mind has always looked for new ways to do things or for a better understanding of old things or for new understanding of what I knew. The fences were simply obstacles that were in the way of making a better me. The fences became challenges unless someone took the time to explain why the fence was there, or explain why I should pay attention to the need to go no further. Even though I have crossed a few fences, I have never been lost. However, I have been reprimanded, sometimes severely.

We can also relate these "fence line stories" to Adam and Eve. They had a similar problem with the forbidden tree. They knew where the fence was, but they pushed the boundary to experience what would happen. If a little pushing was all that resulted, it wouldn't have been such a big deal. But that isn't all that happened.

The fences are there for a reason. We may not know or understand the reason, but reasons exist just the same. For Mike, the fence was there to separate land uses or land owners, but for his sake on that day, the fence was suppose to stop him form going any further and it did. For me in my career, the fences were there to protect the corporation from uninformed utilization of resources and ultimately protection of the owners. Sometimes it took some pushing to find out exactly what the consequences were. I am sure you can understand that in a few instances the consequences were more than I expected.

Not everyone who needs to know the reason for the fences actually does. For Adam and Eve, the fence was there because God wanted to keep his creation close to Him, and He still does. On THAT day, however, God was definitely disappointed. His reaction was severe and so were the consequences both to man and to God.

Although my brother, Mike, wasn't lost, he wasn't where he was supposed to be either. The same is true with God. Although Adam and Eve had crossed the fence, they were not lost; they just were not where they were supposed to be. What God had in mind originally now had to be tempered with the fact that humans had to decide for themselves what was right and what was wrong. God knew mankind couldn't make these decisions without Him. However, God's man creation didn't know that they required assistance in making these decisions. The problem was that mankind had to learn that assistance was available. Mankind had to learn where to get the direction that was needed. Mankind had to learn how the directions would be given. Mankind had to learn that direction could be found if God's help was sought. At least that was what God was hoping when He gave independence to this man creation.

God's assistance is always available but it has to be requested. God knew that humans learn either because they want to or because they have to. God knew that if He tried to teach humans something before they were ready to learn it, they would miss most of the lesson. Just like in the Garden, God constantly teaches us what direction to take our lives. But, also, just like in the Garden, where our desire was to learn more about God's creation, our desires get in the way of that lesson. Only parts of the lesson get through until God throws us into the wilderness and we have to learn the lesson to survive the hard way.

An eternal struggle exists between mankind and God. The struggle is between the temptation to find our own direction and the desire to please God. This struggle also exists between persons and their boss or between a child "driver" and a grownup hunter. We seem to think we know better until we get into trouble, then we have to wait for direction.

I can imagine my Brother Mike's frustration. He did what he was told, but yet nothing happened like his previous experiences. He must have been torn between finding his own way and staying put. At age 11, he knew he had better do as he was told and stay put. Later in his life he would learn the cost of going beyond the fence. He would also find that if the reasons for the fences were well defined, the rewards available for staying within the boundaries were abundant. (These lessons need more room for details that are beyond the point of this story, so we will leave them for another time.)

God knows the struggles we go through in our lives as we try to find the directions we need to exist. God knows that our independence will block the way to the understanding that He wants us to attain. God also knows that we have the resources available to find the correct direction.

We plod along until it dawns on us that God was with us all the time. He was either giving us direction or allowing us to become so lost that the only way out was to ask God for help. Taking God with us is usually not an option we consider at the beginning of our journeys. On those occasions when we take God along from the beginning, what a rewarding experience we have.

One of the aides modern mankind has for assisting us in knowing where we are is GPS (Global Positioning System). I bought my wife a GPS car unit for her birthday. Our recent move into the middle of the Manistee National Forrest was ok with me because I have enjoyed the wilderness all of my life. But for someone who "believes" that all trees look alike and has no sense of direction, moving to the wilderness was like being constantly lost. Even when my wife arrived at a landmark she had recognized on previous journeys, the land mark might make no sense to her. The land mark was really unrecognizable if she encountered it from a different direction that she had never traveled before. Not only did she not know where she was if she was out of sight of our cabin, she would become so frustrated that she would forget where she was going. Now, I am here to tell you, that is lost! A simple walk in the woods was ok with her as long as I was along. And believe you me, she was so attached she clung to me like a "stick-tight". She's a little better about leaving home now that she has her GPS. She is still learning that every road leads somewhere. Leave it to her, however, she argues with the GPS about which direction to take. The GPS just shuts off and waits for her to reprogram it.

The consequence of being thrown into the wilderness caused Adam and Eve to learn that if they wanted to find the right direction, they needed to take the first step. The GPS is the same. The GPS knows where we are, but unless we take a step in some direction, it doesn't know whether we are going in the right direction or the wrong. God knows where we are. He also is always available to assist with finding the right direction. But, we have to take the first step. We have to be the one who makes a move. We have to be the one who sets our sights on the object of our desires before God can step in and help. Even then, we have to be the one to ask for assistance. I believe that God can do things without us but He would much rather that we went along with His plan. He doesn't know where we are in that plan until we make a move and ask Him to come along. He is confident that the talents He has given us will make it possible for us to choose the way to His plan.

God's creation has so many facets, that it is easy to become distracted. God's direction is sometimes very hard to discern because we allow the distractions to side track us. Convincing ourselves that we are on the right track is a constant human pastime. Sometimes we take the trek simply because we think the trail is easier. Other times we take the trek because we don't know any better and failed to ask for help. God has given us plenty of road signs. The direction He wants us to follow has plenty of room for adventure. We only need to keep our mind set on the fact that He is the Creator and He is the one who receives the glory for our actions.

In this instance of finding the correct direction, there are no consequences to God if you don't follow His route. He cares and does not want to loose our souls. He will be disappointed when we become lost just like He was when Adam and Eve ate the forbidden fruit. The path we follow may become loaded with hard work, pain, and discomfort, but these are of no consequence to God. The price of not paying attention to God's GPS comes out of our pockets, not His. He is the Creator no matter what. What more can God do? What is standing in the way of our reception of the correct directions? What more is required of Him to provide the directions we need?

After all, think about what God has given us. I call His gifts the five "T's"; time, thought, treasure, trust, and talent. These gifts are not hard to understand. The presence of these gifts in our lives is constantly before us. All we have to do is think about the impact that these gifts have in our existence; to understand them; and the direction they give us.

The motto my high school graduating class had, "The short span of life is long enough for living well and honorably"[1], says it all with respect to time. The time God has given us is enough. God has given us all of the thought we need. Just look at our very existence. If our creation isn't proof enough, just think about all that we know. All of the treasures we need came from God. Just look around and enjoy the beauty of God's creation and the people who surround us. And trust? Just think about the fact that God leaves us alone until we ask for His help. All of the talent we need has come from God. We just have to use it for His good. Just think of the capabilities we have.

Being lost has no excuse. Even if you are momentarily confused, the path that God wants us to follow can be found. If we find ourselves hopelessly confused, stop a minute and look around. God, and fellow man with God's assistance, is available to help. There is always one way to get back on the right path and it doesn't cost a thing.

REFERENCES

1. Muskegon Senior High School, Muskegon, Michigan, 1959

DISCUSSION QUESTIONS

1. What is your reaction when you run into a fence?
2. Are you ever lost, or do you usually know the way?
3. What do you do when your personal GPS needs to be reprogrammed?

THE CONSEQUENCES

CHAPTER 18

Who's Afraid Of The Big Bad Wolf?
Who Turned Out The Lights?

The bliss of ignorance is a shallow shield
When fighting the evil to get God's will to yield.

Our world was full of consequences that we could never have imagined after being in the lap of luxury that the Garden offered. One of those consequences was fear. In the Garden, Adam and Eve had no reason for fear. God was responsible for everything. Like innocent babes, they were cradled in God's creation with no reason to ever consider anything could be dangerous to them, real or imaginary. Fear was non-existent until their ill fated apple break and God threw them into the wilderness.

New experiences resulted from being on their own. They learned that they could be harmed. They learned that injuries occurred because of their lack of concern for their surroundings or because of the careless actions of others. They learned about death and it frightened them. They were told that if they ate the fruit from the tree of knowledge of good and evil that they would die, but they didn't know what dieing meant. It didn't take long. Cain, Adam and Eve's first born son, taught them in short order when he killed his brother Able[2], Adam and Eve's second born son.

We have many different names for our fears. If you go on line to *phobiaslist.com*[3], I am certain that you will understand what I mean. The phobia list site teaches us that since the word "phobia" is Greek, it is proper to connect the word phobia to another Greek word in order to coin a new phobia. After writing 17 chapters about Adam and Eve and the forbidden fruit, I guess I have to say that one of the phobias I don't have is "logophobia".

This basic human emotion, "fear", had to start somewhere. I can't help but wonder whether or not fear would be part of our emotional make up if Adam and Eve had not taken that bite of the forbidden fruit. Probably not! So, I guess this emotion is another consequence of being thrown into the wilderness. Was there fear in the Garden of Eden? Again, probably not! As proof, Eve went forward with her desire to find out about the knowledge of good and evil without displaying any sign of fear despite being told that she would die if she did.

It's interesting that this emotion is ingrained into our nervous system as an instinct upon birth. This response to danger or unsafe conditions is part of our desire to survive. In some cases, we even thrive on the emotion.

Our phobias cause us to respond out of proportion to real danger. Even worse, though, the fears that result, in some instances, permits others to gain control over our actions. Security versus fear seems to be as powerful as good versus evil. In fact, I know situations exist where we will let evil win because we fear the consequences of threats against our security or perceived security. We find security in our job; security in our home; and security in our comfort with what we believe about God and Christ. "Thou shalt not invade these realms of existence."

When I was a teenager, the house where we lived was a small two bedroom home, and I mean small! In fact the living room was a converted porch. Just to make this more interesting, I was the oldest of four siblings. As the family grew larger, it became necessary for my brother and I to move to a makeshift bedroom in the basement. In my senior year in high school, the City of Muskegon (Michigan) undertook an urban development project that eliminated our home. Our house was designated to be destroyed and required us to move. I can remember my parents grumbling and carrying on about these "unnecessary city actions". One comment in particular stands out in my mind when my stepfather couldn't understand why the planners objected to his red shingled lean-to that was next to the house. It was singled out in a public meeting as an example of the need for the neighborhood to be redeveloped. He took considerable pride in that lean-to. He had built it specifically to store his new boat so that it would be convenient for him to hook up and go fishing. After all, it was on the alley side of the house, what was it hurting? The fear of having to relocate after spending 10 years in this house was extremely frustrating. Once we moved, we couldn't help but wonder why we hadn't moved before we had outgrown the house in the first place.

It seems that is the way with fear. We often blow the emotion way out of proportion in comparison to the real consequences. On the other hand, we can not neglect that the sensation that fear creates is real. I have a very close friend who would give you the shirt off his back if you needed it. He visited us here at our "wilderness home" before we had made it our home. The house is close to the South Branch of the Pere Marquette River. I was looking forward to showing him "my river" when he visited. There is a location not too distant from the cabin where we could drive and catch a view of it from on top of a hill overlooking a gorgeous scene with the river wandering below our feet on a steep sandy bank. He wouldn't even get out of the car.

Fear of heights; fear of closed spaces; fear of the number thirteen; fear of black cats; fear of walking under ladders; on and on we can go. No doubt about it, these irrational fears can limit our ability to experience some of God's greatest creations.

Those of us who don't have these obvious fears have a difficult time understanding the out of proportion response. Just because we have managed to identify a phobia in someone else, we don't have the right to judge the irrationality. We all have our phobias and we all hope like hell that no one finds them out.

There is another aspect of fear that I have never learned to appreciate, the exhilarating chill that some people experience when they go out of their way to experience danger or submit their senses to an element of horror. I have never had a desire to challenge some adventures just to raise the hair on the back of my neck. Purposely going out of my way to put myself in the way of harm in order to experience the joy and excitement of fear has never been an adventure that I have challenged. On the other hand, I have done some things in my life that others would say do just that very thing. I ride motorcycles; I started and successfully ran my own business; I enjoy public speaking (apparently glossophobia is one of the most profound phobias that people can have); and I am not afraid to climb a ladder once I get started. Yet, the thrill aspect of fear has never excited me into experiencing it on purpose.

Out of all of the consequences, I can think of, that have resulted from Eve taking that first bite of the forbidden fruit, fear seems to be the most profound. It is the one sensation that drives us furthest from God. Not only do we not like others to find out what our fears are, we also try to hide them from God. Why do you suppose that is? Perhaps it is because we believe that fear for the most part is the result of our creation, not God's. Although it is hard to convince most of us that fear is a state of mind, deep down we know that the feeling of anxiety that results from fear is basically from our own making. Oh yes, there is no doubt that the fear is real. It is nearly impossible to imagine a world without fear. Yet, God did not create fear. God created life. Fear was created out of desperation once man found out that he was not immortal.

I am reminded of a story about a bird, a Russian farmer, and a fox. One cold winter day, a Russian farmer was driving his troika into town to get supplies when he came across a bird suffering from the cold. The farmer decided to help the bird, being the good person that he was. As he was wondering how to help the bird, one of the horses in the troika defecated. The farmer reasoned that he could put the bird in that pile of manure to get warm. So the farmer put the bird in the manure and continued on his way to town to complete his errand. Sure enough, the bird began to feel better. In fact, the bird felt so much better that he began to sing. About that time a fox came along looking for dinner. When he heard the bird, well, you can imagine what happened next.

Now that is the end of the story, but the story has three morals: 1) It isn't always your enemies that get you into trouble; 2) it isn't always your friends that get you out; 3) but once you find yourself in a bunch of "crap", don't go around singing about it.

Obviously, that bird had nothing to fear about the fox until it was too late. Oftentimes we are that way as well. We don't realize we are in a situation that could harm us until it is too late. Then fear sets in and we react. Nothing is as bleak as waking up and finding yourself in a situation that at first glance seems hopeless.

Not too long ago, I suffered an illness that resulted in a need for me to learn how to walk, talk, swallow, roll over, and stand up all over again. This illness has physically kept me from doing all of the things that I truly have enjoyed doing all of my life. The results still restrict many of the activities that I use to be good at doing. I was unconscious for more than six weeks and was in the hospital for 110 days. I can't begin to tell you the fear I had when I regained consciousness. I didn't know what had happened to me. I had no idea of the turmoil that my family had gone through while I was unconscious. When I came to, I could only remember what life was like before I became ill and wonder what had gone wrong. The doctors told my wife that if I hadn't checked myself into the walk-in clinic, she would have found me dead when she got home from work that day.

The fear I experienced about the outcome was unbelievable. I had no idea what was going to happen next. I had no control over anything. I had to push the call button just to get help to roll over in bed. The smallest wrinkle in the sheets caused excruciating pain to my back. The nurses teased me about being as bad as the princess and the pee[1]. As I lay in the darkness night after night trying to recover, the darkness of the night was not my concern. The darkness in my spirit became deeper and deeper as I tried to imagine how I was going to make my way to the surface from this deep despair.

Three things happened that caused me to rise above the darkness. First, my family, especially my wife; but my children, my brothers and my sister were always there to provide moral support and bring relief from the darkness. Secondly, I was in a Catholic hospital and a crucifix hung on the wall in my limited viewing range. It reminded me of the ultimate sacrifice made for me and the darkness in mankind that was overcome with that sacrifice. Lastly, a voice from a member of the clergy employed at the hospital that crept into my consciousness one night telling me that if I needed to be released from the anxiety of my situation that she was there to talk and we did.

That experience taught me about the depths of despair and the darkness of fear. It also taught me that a resource exists that is just waiting to be invited to help bring light to the darkest of situations. I have recovered much of what I lost with the help of friends, doctors, nurses, therapists, family, and just plain stubbornness. But most of all the help has come from the love that God has for me and His creation.

The darkness that surrounds fear is only there because we prevent the light of God's love from shinning in these recesses of our minds. In fact, I would venture, that most of us do not know how to let that light penetrate those fear recesses. When we are in the middle of the darkness that surrounds fear, the first thing we think of is not the light of the love of God! The first thing we think of is how the hell did we get ourselves into this situation? The second thing we think of is how the hell do we get ourselves out? Then, maybe, the next thing we think of is; "Please God help me make the best of this situation".

REFERENCES

1. A story by Hans Christian Andersen about a prince that sought a "real' princess and found her because of her ability to feel a pee even though it was on a mattress twenty mattress layers below.
2. Genesis 4:8
3. A listing of phobia terms and their meaning.

DISCUSSION QUESTIONS

1. What is your greatest fear?
2. Are fears real or self-imposed?
3. Do you seek GOD's wisdom and compassion to help you overcome your fears?

THE CONSEQUENCES

CHAPTER 19

What Is Your Problem? Who Am I Hurting?

*Copping an attitude is a common ploy
For those who seek relationships to destroy.*

The daunting task of learning how to get along with one another is one consequence of learning the difference between good and evil that still confounds us. God's tough love lesson seems to set us on edge with each other as we try to find a way back into God's good graces. Just like kids, we fight for His attention and usually when we receive it, the results are not what we were expecting. That act of separation when God threw Adam and Eve out of the Garden has left mankind in a situation where dependence on each other becomes a key to successful existence. Yet, we can't seem to harmonize with the effort. Instead, each of us thinks our way is better than anybody else's. We posture, we act, we sing, we snarl, we grumble, we praise, we cuss, and we swear. Oh yes, we try to overcome our differences, but we always seem to put our interest first. Maybe that is why all of us have so few really true friends.

Even with friends, we associate best with those who basically share our attitude about other people, politics, living conditions and other circumstances. When the situation becomes dire and we obviously need to change something to suit our needs better, the circle of "friends" either broadens or diminishes as we develop the solution. Some of us are mellower than others, know more about diplomacy, and can handle troublesome situations better than others. Yet, there always seems to be somebody whose attitude defies diplomacy. What seems right and good to one person is offensive and evil to another person. I have even seen situations where two people with different opinions used the same Bible verse to justify their position on a confusing matter. Not only that, the matter was so ridiculous, no real consequence resulted to anyone; at least that is what I thought.

Human nature seems to bristle at the possibility that the way we are thinking requires correction. In some situations significant convincing is necessary to change ones mind. Even then, we have to find some way to "save face" so that our ego isn't deflated too severely. Other times, when we are on the "winning side", we can't let bygones be bygones. Instead, we adopt an attitude that is just a smidgeon less than "I told you so". How do we get off this one-up-man-ship trolley with an understanding that appreciates both sides?

Can you imagine having a situation where over half of a church family was at odds over such a trivial matter as coffee? In Chapter 10 we discussed how members argued "good and evil" for weeks about having coffee in the sanctuary during church service. This simple mater was a new idea trying to reach out to the community of non-church goers in a friendly down-home gesture to join us for coffee on Sunday morning during a contemporary service. My word! You would have thought that the devil himself had taken a hold of some of us and we were trying to send everyone to hell. The ones complaining the most were well respected strong believing individuals in the church community. They couldn't accept the "sacrilegious" atmosphere being fostered with the privilege of bringing a cup of coffee into the sanctuary. It was of such concern to them that they believed they couldn't worship properly.

During a meeting to settle the issue, the pastor changed his position on the matter and a ruling was made to not allow coffee in the sanctuary. Needless to say, this decision caused several individuals to back way off their involvement in their church activity. Unfortunately they were the principal drivers for the out reach project. None of the group disallowing the coffee stepped forward to fill the needs for the involvement so the out reach effort basically died. Not only that, the ruling had no accountability, no policemen appointed to enforce the ruling; so people brought coffee in the sanctuary anyway. Nose cutting, spite, and face issues come to mind. What was evil to one was good to someone else. Sorting this out required the wisdom of Solomon[1], but at the time of the meeting, Solomon was unavailable and no one seemed to have enough wisdom to substitute for him, including me. Although I was in favor of the outreach objective of the "for coffee" group and voted for the proposal, I understood the inability of accepting a "coffee distraction" in the sanctuary. It seems to me, however, if more people are going to be reached with the word of God if coffee was allowed in the sanctuary for the contemporary service, than allow the coffee.

Our desire to be individuals together seems to make us think that together we can't be individuals. Being separated from God just because Adam and Eve listened to the snake and took that big bite has definitely caused considerable turmoil as we try to make things right with God for ourselves.

Individually, we don't seem to have a problem talking with God. We might have a problem listening to Him, but talking with Him, no problem. For some people, talking with God is part of their every day language as they ask for God's damning powers. We find that we can talk with God about many situations and many issues as long as we don't have to listen to His answer. Other times we hear His answer but can't believe what He is telling us. Sometimes we don't receive an answer, at least that we can recognize, only to later realize that was His answer. And still other times we willingly listen to his answer because the answer is exactly what we thought it should be.

If we could only recognize that God is talking to us all of the time, that His directions are worth listening to all of the time, and maybe, just maybe, the pleasures of living with each other could be realized.

Too bad we can't talk with each other like we can manage to talk with God. Please keep in mind that I have said "talk". I have said nothing about "listening". Even the talking with each other will never happen completely, just like it doesn't happen with God, because of the listening part. We pretend not to hear, but people know we are listening, and God knows we are listening as well. We have learned to interpret what they say even when they didn't say it. Body language, voice inflections, gesticulation, even attitudes are communication devices that ring loud and clear in every conversation. Too bad we can't "see" God when we try talking with Him. On top of all those other issues, add the defensive baggage each of us carry religiously as we go from situation to situation just to make certain that no one hurts us **AGAIN**. This baggage prevents us from fully appreciating and understanding the other side. I suppose that we carry God baggage as well, but we are afraid to admit it since we know that God knows best.

Fortunately, there is good baggage as well! It is amazing how the synergistic effects of good intentions can deploy to accomplish a task that would never be completed, if it depended on individual efforts. The difference between success and failure of good intentions is ownership. It seems to me that the daunting task of getting along is finding a way for everyone to participate with the skills that they have. People make things happen because of their talents and capabilities as long as they are allowed to use them and be recognized for their contribution. Leaders lead. Teachers teach. Engineers engineer. Workers work. Writers write. Finding something for everyone allows the good baggage to be used. Allowing everyone to have their input, if they want it, works wonders (sometimes).

In my opinion, for some reason, the news media believes we don't know how to listen. I really don't know where they ever developed that notion. It is amazing to me that they believe they have a lock on listening correctly. For example, they spend hours telling us what the President said in a forty five minute speech. Of course, they make a living at doing the listening for us so maybe we ought to take a few lessons from them. **NOT!** The freedom of the press doesn't require the press to remove any bias. The freedom of the press doesn't require the press to report all of the news. The freedom of the press doesn't require the press to present all of the interpretations. The freedom of the press doesn't require the press to consider any moral damage it might be fostering. The freedom of the press doesn't require the press to be responsible for any commotion it creates intentionally or unintentionally. Freedom of choice doesn't require any of these considerations either. Maybe that is the problem! If we mix these considerations into our choices, the wisdom that is discussed in Proverbs might, just might, come to pass.

I like making bread. Some of my bread making experiences can be used to exemplify these notions I am trying to explain. I make bread the old fashioned way, using my hands rather than a bread machine. When I make bread, I usually make somewhere between twelve and fifteen loaves. As a consequence, I give a lot of bread away. On more than one occasion, I have had individuals request bread and I usually have a lot of fun meeting their request. I must admit, though, that many of the ideas I use came from my father-in-law who also made bread. Both of us became involved with making bread because of "our suggestions" to our wives when they were making the bread. We were simply told, "If you have a better idea, make it yourself." My wife hasn't made bread in nearly forty years.

I remember one individual who commented to my father-in-law that the bread didn't have enough salt to satisfy him. The next time my father-in-law made bread, this individual received a special loaf. The bread dough was wrapped around a box of salt before the dough raised and the bread was baked. The box of salt was hidden inside. You can imagine what I have done with raisin bread when I was told that it didn't have enough raisins and the same issue with caraway seeds in rye bread. Neither one of us has ever sold a loaf. When asked, we have simply stated that if we charged for it, then they would have something to complain about so we don't.

What is it about human nature that causes us to ignore or, at the very least, to be insensitive to how others will be affected by our actions? In many instances, we hold our tongue so that we don't offend people. We are not born with this trait. Some of us take a lot longer to learn the trait than others, however. That is a good thing, or maybe it isn't, I can't always tell. The Book of Proverbs[2] is full of advice for seeking wisdom and not being foolish. How do we put this advice to good use in every situation? What prompts us to ignore the advice when we know darn good and well that we ought to be using it? Freedom of choice, knowledge of good and evil, separation from God, the desire to get back in God's good graces; something is driving us to distraction; but distraction from what? The distraction must be the separation.

God threw mankind out of the Garden, but His love for His creation has never ceased. So who is separated from whom? The separation is in our conscience. We would like to believe that we are all basically good people just seeking to find a way to exist without having guilty feelings about the way we interact with other human beings. Oh, I will grant you that there are truly bad people out there who have given their soul to the devil. Most of us, however, are trying to get along, with our foolishness and lack of wisdom blocking the way now and then. Just like knowledge begins with respect for the Lord[3], so does wisdom[4].

At this point, though, I have a "yabut". <u>Yes, but (yabut)</u> how do we find the right way? The answer is to seek God's way, not your way. If we could only think about the Creator and creation in those moments when we seem to be confused about the difference between good and evil, most of our confusion would be eliminated. Easier said than done in the heat of the moment, I know! Easier said than done in any moment as a matter of fact! Such an ideal world might exist somewhere, but it is a long way from existing for most of us.

REFERENCES

1. 1 King 3: 7—12
2. Proverbs is a "book" in the Bible
3. Proverbs 1 v. 7
4. Proverbs 9 v.10

DISCUSSION QUESTIONS

1. Is it your way or the highway?
2. Why do we not allow ourselves to compromise?
3. When you speak to GOD, do you think HIS arms are crossed or wide open?

THE CONSEQUENCES

CHAPTER 20

Who Is That In The Mirror On The Wall? Is It Me?

What visage is it that I see?
Is it really the one I want to be?

In this day and age, identity theft seems to run rampant. My grandson and I went to a well-known men's clothing store the other day to order tuxedos. He was ordering his for a prom. I was ordering mine for an award event I was attending. I paid for mine with a credit card. My grandson paid for his with a debit card. He rarely used his debit card because he rarely has money in his account to debit against. In this particular instance having limited funds in his account was a good thing. The following evening, the bank called him to alert him to some unusual activity on his account. Apparently, someone was using his card to buy plane tickets, internet songs, and a few other items. The total had exceeded his balance and the bank doing what it is supposed to do, called to be certain that the charges were legitimate. Of course they weren't and he had to go to the bank the following day to identify which purchases were not his and to change his account number. Boy, what a hassle. In the meantime, he called the clothing store to alert the manager to what had happened. He made certain that he didn't accuse the clothing store. He pointed out that the clothing store was the last place he had used his debit card and that he had not used his card for several weeks prior to the occasion when he rented the tuxedo. Of course, the manager thanked him and declared he would look into it. We don't know what happened after that.

We all know that if someone were to steal our identity, it would be a big inconvenience to straighten everything out. But what is it they are stealing? It is nothing but a bunch of numbers, which, unfortunately, allow us access to what is our accumulated existence on this earth. To a certain extent, our identity is our reputation and the numbers vouch for our wealth and how trustworthy we are. They show how much money we have at our disposal; they show how well we have paid back our debts; and they show what money we have coming to us. This identity is mostly related to money. People who steal our identity desire to take advantage of who we are and what we have accredited to our existence. These identity thefts are for monetary gain at the expense of some one who has earned the benefits that are being stolen. It is all for monetary purposes.

Have you ever stopped to consider, if identity theft wasn't for monetary gain what do you have that would be worth stealing? Considering this aspect even further, if you had something else other than monetary gain worth stealing, how would they steal it. A significant amount of work has gone into the identity that describes who you are and what you have become. I would venture to say that most of us would have a hard time describing ourselves even if we could look into a mirror. Certainly, the image that is reflected has a description, but does that reflection really show who we are and what we stand for? I don't think so.

Recently, I had an opportunity to evaluate myself for my employer. I haven't done that is several years. I have, on the other hand asked my employees to perform a self-evaluation of themselves in preparation for annual raises. The form that I had for my employees was made for me to perform the evaluation, not the employee. However, I always asked the employee to do the evaluation first. That way I had something to go by. Nothing like having the people that work for you do your work. Besides, I have always found that my employees were harder on themselves than I ever was.

When my evaluation was completed this time, low and behold, I was harder on myself than the boss was. Go figure! The evaluation required me to rate my attitude, my cooperativeness, my enthusiasm, my ability to work on my own, my interactions with others, and probably fifteen other categories. Some of the items had heavier weighting than others. One of the most interesting outcomes was that I scored really high on career development, but was only "Good" on craftsmanship. It seems to me that this is a little backwards. It seems backwards because I am 69 years old and I am only working part time for the people that bought my business. They told me one of the reasons they bought my business was the fact that I had excellent rapport with my client base.

As we look back over our careers, reflecting on how far we have come, one can't help wondering how much influence Snake has had in the choices we have made. I remember a choice I made early in my career between family and work. The choice has haunted me from the day I made it. I was working for a large, very large, company at the time and was anxious to be an active integral part of the corporation. As a consequence, I made a decision to remain at work at a time of mourning in my family. My wife's grandfather had passed away and I believed that it was more important for me to stay at work than to attend his funeral. My wife wouldn't go without me. We had a young family that needed more than her attention in situations like this. I have regretted that decision every since. It wasn't too many years after that when I found a better way. I dedicate my career to my creator. This commitment puts a different perspective on the relationships between God, family, and work. I definitely would make this funeral attendance choice differently today!

The influence that Snake brings to the commitments we make is astounding. When we have a chance to look back and reflect on some of the bad decisions we have made, we find Snake's work. Of course, we can look back at the good decisions we have made just as well and see how we have told Snake to go back to hell where he came from.

Who are we, really? What have we become? Are we what we set out to be? When people see us do they see the image we want them to see or do they see an image we have been hiding? Worse yet, are they blinded by what they have become and only see what they want to see?

The trials and tribulations we face everyday cause us to project images that we think fit the situation. Try as we might, temptations interfere with what we know we want to be and what we know we ought to be to be. We confuse what we are with something we are not, or with something we want to be, or with something that others want us to be. Just as in the Garden of Eden, where Adam and Eve knew what they were supposed to do; we also know what we are supposed to do. The forces of desire to control are far more powerful that most of us are willing to admit.

What a conundrum! We are supposed to know the difference between good and evil. After all we succumbed to the temptation that Snake gave us so that we would know this crucial difference. Yet, we can't seem to get it right especially when it counts the most. We look back and what do we see? Most of us recall those rotten situations that we wish we could do over again. We cringe as we think about actions that were not received as we intended them to be. Those memories can far out weigh the memories of the good things, if we let them.

We wonder, whether the values and morals that represent our understanding of good evil are correct? Have we passed on those values and morals effectively? What has temptation done to us? Do we reflect the values we think we reflect? How do we find out if we are what we set out to be? Some of us will never know. Others will find out that we don't always look in the right places. Still others will simply be completely oblivious to their surroundings. The most unpleasant of these situations occurs when we come to grips with a circumstance where our behavior was judged to be totally unacceptable. The unpleasantness is most severe when this judgment comes from someone whose opinion we value most. The humiliation is mostly in our minds, but it is still there, and it really hurts when it comes from a person that we hold in high esteem.

I can't help with most of these questions, but I can offer some of my own experiences, which may assist those who don't know where to look. I have had many opportunities to reflect on what I have become. Most of the time, I learn from the good-natured kidding that occurs when I am in the company of my children. This kidding is especially meaningful when we are all together. What I have passed on to my children is reflected by what they do, what they say, and how they act.

My children are now grown adults, married and with children of their own. I remember one occasion that allowed me to reflect on what I passed on to them. On this occasion, I received a telephone call from my eldest son thanking me for the sense of value he had concerning the ability to make his own way. Apparently, he had a relative that was not showing the proper appreciation for all that her parents and grandparents had sacrificed to see to it that she and her mother had a place to live and food to eat. As I have already mentioned in a previous chapter, I believe that there are two ways to raise children: one is to have them dependent on me for everything; the other is to encourage them to do for themselves. With the first, the dependence seems to last forever and children are always around even after adulthood. With the other, independence reduces the need for them to hang around, and their need to be near their parents for security is not an issue. Until that time my son had called, I didn't know if the choice I made as a parent was appreciated. It was great to hear that it was!

In a second instance, I really learned what my children thought about me as a parent. I had contracted Legionella and was in the hospital for 110 days. (The same 110 days mentioned in Chapter 18.) Half of that time I was unconscious. When I regained consciousness, I learned how close to death I had been. I also learned what a resource my children were. The eldest came from Atlanta on Fridays and Saturdays to run the financial side of my business. He would also do what he could with the technical end of the business. He is a mechanical engineer and had his own business at one time and had the experience to do these chores. My second eldest came

Thursdays and Fridays from Chicago to help his mother with the household finances. He teaches high school math so this job was easy for him. The youngest, my daughter, came from Grand Rapids during the first part of the week to assist her mother with the insurance issues, which were overwhelming as you might imagine. They all pulled together and spent as much time as they could by my bedside encouraging me to regain my health and strength.

Now, I am not encouraging you to become deathly ill in order to find out if the value system you thought you taught your children was properly learned. However, I am encouraging you to make an effort to teach your children your value system and if you don't have one develop one and teach it. May I suggest that Jesus is one example worth considering? Your children will learn whatever you teach them and sooner or later you will know what it was that you taught them. If you want to see what your value system looks like, look at your children. They look like you in more ways than you think.

Yes, I know, you are thinking how naive I am to believe that my value system, as it relates to good and evil, is the only value system that my children have experienced or will experience and you are correct. Snake can find his way into the tiniest cracks and can offer his subtle ways. He can distract even the best intentions. I have no solutions for those situations except to hold your course. The only person I can control is "me". I have no authority to control others. I have no control over how others receive my intentions. I have no way to be able to convince you that my way and your way are equally acceptable. I can tell you that both our ways are a compilation of exposure to many individuals in our lives. I can also tell you that this compilation is a result of both positive and negative influences. I can also tell you that this compilation is the result of an inherent knowledge of good and evil imparted to us from the very beginning. How we reflect that inherent knowledge totally reflects the images we have adopted from individuals we have held in some esteem during our lives. I can also tell you with confidence that personally, I would rather have that reflection be something I am proud of and not ashamed of. You must understand, I have had both and I am not about to tell you about the evil!

As the years go by, I have also learned that several facets of my existence other than my family have affected my knowledge of good and evil. I have learned, for example, that I have a desire to know more and to understand more so that I can be more definitive with regard to the choices I make concerning good and evil. This desire to have a better understanding sometimes exasperates me as well as the people with whom I associate. At times I want to be like the child that asks "why" no matter what the answer is. It seems like I am constantly on the verge of understanding some great revelation and just at the instant it is about to disclose itself, it disappears like a wisp. My faith continues to grow, as does my understanding of my faith. One of the most revealing aspects of my faith occurred while I was recovering from the Legionella, when my wife told me about her encounters with doctors who asked if they could pray with her as they had done all they could. My wife's philosophy of "what good is faith if you can't use it" took on a whole new meaning for me. I remembered there is another aspect of faith. In addition to the faith we have in God, God has faith in us as well. He believes you can do the job he has set out for us otherwise he wouldn't have given you the task in the first place!

DISCUSSION QUESTIONS

1. What part of your personality is worth stealing?
2. Are you a "what you see is what you get" person, or do you only expose parts of yourself and hide the rest?
3. If you could have one "do-over", what would it be?

THE CONSEQUENCES

CHAPTER 21

Am I Good Or What? It Is All About Me, Isn't It? Is This All For Me?

Thinking we have done it all the right way
Forgets that God might have something to say!

From the time I had my first job transplanting celery seedlings in a hot house for 50¢ a thousand at the ripe old age of 13 until now; I have had an innate sense of independence. That independence coupled with my pragmatic upbringing from a stepfather that didn't graduate from 9th grade has left me with a confidence attitude second to none. My step father wasn't afraid to tackle any task that involved nuts and bolts or machining. However, I also have been left with an attitude that if I can do it, anybody can! The consequence is that I have unjust expectations of others. It is easy for me to have little patience with people who have difficulty understanding how things go together and how they do what they do. My wife has asked me more than once about how I learned to do the things I can do. I can't really answer that question, but I can tell you that I have had frequent occasions where I should have hired a professional! I have screwed up more fundamental repairs than I care to think about. On the other hand, my handyman abilities have allowed me to fix many broken household devices and pay less for many of these jobs than most people. I will say, of all of these tasks, "I hate plumbing!"

I don't know how long Adam and Eve were in the garden before Snake came along, but it isn't hard to imagine that they had been there without supervision for some time. After all, they were essentially on their own and Adam had been busy with his notepad and Sharpie naming all of the flora and fauna, so I am certain they had developed some degree of independence. If God was anything like He is today, He probably wasn't hovering over their every move either. In fact I truly believe He wasn't present for a good share of the time, otherwise He wouldn't have needed to issue His warning about the tree of knowledge of good and evil. Without supervision, Adam and Eve most likely developed a certain degree of independence just like most of us do.

The Old Testament is full of God events where people seemingly left alone have turned to their own devises. The most notorious one was when Moses came down from the mountain with the Ten Commandments the first time[1], but over and over again, the Old Testament people loose touch with God and do something stupid that is not in keeping with what God intended. Just like Eve, sooner or later they get curious and think that they know more than God and they take action in accordance with what is familiar to them, or even more dangerously their action is totally without regard for what they know is right.

Even when God is busy doing miracles on our behalf, we seem to find excuses to turn our focus to what <u>we</u> know how to do rather than what God wants us to do. I look at poor Moses and think what does a guy have to do to convince "the chosen people" that they have God on their side? It seems that just like "the chosen people" we need to have God doing a personal miracle for us every day to convince us that He hasn't forgotten us. Even worse, we tell God that if He doesn't show up and save our lousy hides and do what we ask, we will find our own way.

Such mixed signals! God gives us talents to make our way through His creation and then when we use our talents to exercise our independence we find that we should have been relying on God. We think that God isn't there when we need Him the most. We think that as long as His personal touch isn't being felt, we must somehow perform the task without Him. Then we justify our actions by blaming God for not being there. We justify by indicating that He shouldn't have shown us the path, if He didn't want us to follow it. We justify by thinking that, if He didn't want us to do the task ourselves, he shouldn't have given us that choice. Ya right, God, it is your fault entirely. Even Adam blamed God[2].

It seems to me that our spiritual lives take on the same degree of defiance. If we can't get first hand insights from God, we go exploring. We listen for others to provide explanations that make sense to us instead of listening to what we know God is saying because God's way is too difficult. Or we step aside and let others who are speaking louder take the lead despite the fact that we know they are speaking for their own benefit rather than on God's behalf. Worse yet, we let others who we think have studied God's word speak for us. Then we find that our convictions are more in tune with our understanding of God's word than the other person. Just because that person has a position of authority, it dosen't mean he knows more about your situation than you do.

The point is that we think we know better only because we think we have been doing all of the work to develop the understanding. We don't give any credit to God for His part in the creation. Just because we "know the Bible" doesn't mean that we "know" the Bible. Look at the history that is included in the Bible and see how many times God became disgusted when His creation defied His plans. Even when His chosen people benefited directly from His intervention, they couldn't be convinced that God's way was better than their way. They whined; they built idols from what God had given them; they even said that they preferred slavery compared to the "hardships" they were enduring as a consequence of gaining their freedom a short time before. How thankless and unappreciative can we get? Just read some of the prophets in the Old Testement[3] and you will see how disappointed God can get. This is especially true of Jeremiah and Ezekiel just 600 years before Christ was born. God's disgust was so great about what his chosen people were doing that He minced no words over what He was going to do and in fact did[4,5].

If you don't think that you can make God angry (or piss God off as I said in an earlier chapter), you have another thought coming. ("Having another thought coming" was one of my mother's favorite sayings when she wasn't happy with what I was doing. For example she would say, "If you think you can get away with that, you have another thought coming." And then she would show me, usually with a physical reprimand.) You may think that God's creation is just for you, but you still have another thought coming. God's creation is for God and you better be thinking about how God wants you to use it. Free sex is not the way, ask Ezekiel[6]. Man made idols with God made materials is not the way, ask both Ezekiel[7] and Jeremiah[8]. Worshipping those man made idols is not the way either, ask Moses[9]. And if you don't think you can piss off God, ask the Israelites who were captured and sent to Babylon[10] or the Israelites who wandered for forty years in the desert just a few short miles from the Promised Land[11].

Adam and Eve were only the first to disappoint God with their disobedience. Since then, there certainly hasn't been a shortage of people who think they can go it on their own. How many times is it going to take to convince us God's creation is for God and we are not God! How many times is it going to take to convince us that God's creation is not for us? How many times is it going to take to convince us that it's God's way not our way? Examples after example are before us, yet we continue to believe we know how to do it without God. Not only that, we think we can do it better than God!!!! How much more foolish can we get? I hate to keep asking these questions. Somehow, though, I think that we just need to sit down and contemplate how badly we have screwed things up. I can't seem to accomplish this contemplation without asking questions that draw attention to our inadequacies, mine included!

I think that one of the most difficult tasks we have as faith people is to trust God. Jesus told Thomas that if it took him to see the nail holes to believe, then "Blessed are those who have not seen and yet have come to believe."[12]. We live in a world full of deception, so doubting is rather easy. No wonder we lose faith and rely on what we believe to be true. In most instances what we believe is what we know we can do. We forget that what we can do is the result of the talents that the Creator has given us in the first place. By the same token, then, we shouldn't think that God is upset with us for using our God given talents to take care of ourselves.

So, if we think about the talents we have, what is the difference between depending on ourselves and depending on God? What is the difference between thinking about the fun we can have in God's creation and the fun that God wants us to have in his creation? What is the difference between enjoying the opportunities we have with God's creation and the opportunities God want us to enjoy with his creation? What is the difference between thinking we are the center of the universe and being one of God's creatures in His universe? What is the difference between thinking that God's creation is for our personal use and that we are privileged to have His creation at our disposal rather than thinking that His creation is intended for all to use? What is the difference? The difference is a higher level of our awareness as the song "This is My Father's World"[13] says.

I also think that Job[14] had a similar problem. When he started questioning his faith and began contemplating all of the advice his "friends"[14], Eliphaz, Bildad, Zophar, Elihu, were giving him, he became convinced that he needed a "one on one"[15] conversation with God to get the matter straightened out. At least Job didn't lose perspective of who it was that was to receive the benefits of this "living thing"[16]. Oh yes, he eventually got to the level where questioning what this "living thing" was all about became an obsession, but he still stood fast in his righteousness. No wonder he was taken aback when God finally responded. God's response was nowhere near answering the questions Job was raising. Just look at God's response[17]:

> "Then the LORD answered Job out of the whirlwind: ²'Who is this that darkens counsel by words without knowledge? ³Gird up your loins like a man, I will question you, and you shall declare to me. ⁴'Where were you when I laid he foundation of the earth? Tell

me, if you have understanding. ⁵Who determined its measurements—surely you know! Or who stretched the line upon it? ⁶On what were its bases sunk, or who laid its cornerstone ⁷when the morning stars sang together and all the heavenly beings* shouted for joy?

⁸'Or who shut in the sea with doors when it burst out from the womb?—⁹when I made the clouds its garment, and thick darkness its swaddling band, ¹⁰and prescribed bounds for it, and set bars and doors, ¹¹and said, "Thus far shall you come, and no farther, and here shall your proud waves be stopped"?

...

40¹And the LORD said to Job: ²"Shall a fault-finder contend with the Almighty?* Anyone who argues with God must respond."'

I don't know about you, but if God ever responded to me in my anguish like he responded to Job, He would have my attention, forever! So, my final question for this chapter is what is stopping me from giving Him my full attention? For that matter, what is stopping you? Hasn't He already responded?

One last thought! When I think a little further about this matter concerning the "living thing" being all about me, I believe I have come to understand it is all about trust. Solomon had some advice for us about trust:

"Trust the Lord with all your heart, and don't depend on your own understanding. Remember the Lord in all you do, and he will give you success. Don't depend on your own wisdom. Respect the Lord and refuse to do wrong."[18]

REFERENCES

1. Exodus 32:9 – 10
2. Genesis 3:12
3. Isaiah, Jeremiah, Ezekiel, and Ezra Books in the Bible Old Testament
4. Jeremiah 34:2 – 5
5. Ezekiel 23:36 – 48
6. Ezekiel 23:1 – 21
7. Ezekiel 22:3
8. Jeremiah 10:1 – 22
9. Exodus 32:19 – 20
10. Ezekiel 23:22 – 31
11. Numbers 14:32
12. John 23:29
13. "This Is My Father's World" a hymn with words by Maltbie D. Babcock, 1901, While a pastor in Lockport, New York
14. Bible Book Of Job in Old Testament
15. Job 31:35
16. Job 38 v 1 – 40 v 2
17. Job 12:10
18. Proverbs 3: 5 – 7

DISCUSSION QUESTIONS

1. Do you face your dilemmas alone, or with GOD at your side?
2. If you had to knock at the door to heaven today, would anyone answer?
3. "How Great Thou Art" - do you live by it?

THE CONSEQUENCES

CHAPTER 22

Can I Get A Drink Around Here?
Is It Too Much To Ask To Get Something To Eat?

What good is faith if you don't use it?
God will provide as long as you don't abuse it.

Mark Twain once said "Faith is believing what you know ain't so[1]." Faith is also trusting God to provide for all of our needs. Adam and Eve's faith was so simple; they had no reason to believe "it wasn't so". They had no wants; they had no needs. They really didn't even know what faith was. After all, they were on first name speaking terms with God. Yet they took that fateful step, listened to the snake, and tested their belief to determine if God really meant what He said. What really happened to cause Eve (and Adam) to perform this act isn't clear. Chapter 1 of this book discusses some possibilities.

Faith in the Garden was one thing, but think about the faith they needed once they were kicked out of the Garden. Where was the sustenance going to come from? How was shelter going to be provided? Was water readily available outside of the Garden? God vanquished them to a life of hard work. Basically, God said, "If you are going to test Me, I will give you something to test Me about!" At the moment Adam and Eve were thrust into the wilderness, faith was born. Suddenly, they had to have faith in their God given talents to be able to exist at all.

In 2005, I contracted legionella. This was the reason for the 110days in the hospital mentioned in Chapters 18 and 21. Legionella is a potentially fatal illness that develops from an air born bacteria that concentrates in dark moist locations. People don't easily survive the devastating consequences that this illness causes. First, extreme severe pneumonia occurs; then it attacks other vital organs; and finally it attacks and consumes muscle mass. I was in the hospital for 110 days. I don't remember the first 6 weeks due to an induced coma from the need to insert breathing apparatus and other unpleasant devices into my body orifices to keep me alive. In fact, I didn't have enough orifices and they made new ones. I have a new belly button for feeding and I have a scar on my neck where they had to cut my throat (tracheotomy) to insert a breathing device. In Chapter 18 I discussed how the doctors told my wife that she might have found me dead if I hadn't checked myself into the walk-in clinic. They even asked her to pray with them after they had done all they could that first night. They told her that I was seriously ill and that the rest of the family should be informed, which she had already done. To her surprise, however, they also told her that a higher power more capable than they were was needed to pull me through the struggle and wanted to pray with her. I was a sick puppy and didn't know it.

Think about all of the faith issues that were in play. Faith in the doctors believing they knew what they were doing. Faith in the medications that I was given believing they would fight the effects of the bacteria not knowing what the problem was. Faith I hadn't become a vegetable while being deprived of oxygen because of the pneumonia.

Faith is belief and trust in someone or something. For Christians, it is belief in God the Father, Jesus Christ, and the Holy Spirit. Faith in everyday living requires each of us to believe that others will do their part. Just think about the faith needed for a simple act like turning on a light. Faith that the electricity required to cause the light to illuminate will be generated and available. Faith is required to believe that the light bulb will have sufficient integrity to enable the filament to function. Faith is required to believe that unseen people have done their jobs and worked to provide the electricity and the light bulb. Every aspect of our everyday life and existence is based on faith in others. Perhaps we are more inclined to view this as trust.

Faith in the light switch is one thing. Think about the faith required when you purchase your food and beverages. The growing, the processing, the distribution, the sanitation, the longevity, the availability, and the preparation all require faith in order to believe that the final act of consumption will take place without incident or danger. Every step of the entire operation is performed with more than a smidgeon of faith in the previous step and in the step to come. Jesus told us that if God is so willing to take care of even the birds in the air, we shouldn't be concerned that God wouldn't take care of us as well[2] and He does as long as we do our part.

This illness I had was devastating. It progressed to the point that while I was unconscious, I had to be put on 24-hour dialysis. I am told I started retaining water and blew up to nearly 300lbs. My brothers nicknamed me the Michelin man because I had blown up to such huge proportions. I am also told that decisions to pull the plug were on the brink at least three times while I was unconscious. No one could predict what my existence would be like if I even managed to recover. My family was told to sell my motorcycle because the doctors believed I would never ride again. Well, I have ridden again and hope to ride many more miles as well. But when I regained consciousness, I required assistance for everything. The attack on the muscles was so severe that I could not roll myself over in bed. Every wrinkle in the sheet felt like a ridge of rope. The nurses teased me about being like the princess in the Princess and the Pea[3]. I had to learn how to walk all over again.

The most difficult task was learning how to swallow. In fact this aspect took an additional 6 months after I was released from the hospital and was the primary cause for me loosing enough weight to get down to 159lbs. (I went into the hospital weighing 209lbs.)

The spring following my hospitalization, while I was still recovering, I had an occasion to go fishing with a very good friend, Ollen Baldwin. Getting in and out of the boat with my limited strength was a challenge, especially the getting out part. Ollen thought it would be easier for me to get out of the boat, if he rowed me up to the ladder on the dock. The problem was that my legs weren't strong enough to permit me to hoist myself easily out of the boat. Even just standing up in the boat was a chore since I didn't have the use of handrails or any other means of leverage. However, I managed to stand up and get to the edge of the boat next to the ladder. Once I was at the ladder, I managed to lift my left leg onto the first rung of the ladder. Unfortunately, I forgot that although I was able to lift my left leg higher than my right leg, my right leg was stronger than the left one. The problem was that after I managed to get my left leg onto the ladder, I couldn't lift the rest of me up and I couldn't get my leg down once I got it on the ladder. I was in a fix and I couldn't get out of it.

Ollen had to leave the oars and come and give me a boost. Unfortunately, the boat wouldn't hold still for all of this and it slipped sideways with my one foot on the ladder and the rest of me hanging on the best that I could. Finally, with Ollen's help, I managed to sprawl on my belly onto the dock. Ollen got out of the boat, helped me roll over, and sat me up. I had both feet on the top rung of the ladder. Then he helped me stand up and finished hoisting me onto the dock. Meanwhile the boat escaped. Anyone watching, would have thought some strange "goings ons" were taking place on that dock. Think about the faith issue at work in this incident. Faith in my friend's ability to hoist me up; faith in me to tell him what was needed to accomplish the tasks because he couldn't understand what my dilemma was; faith that the flimsy ladder would put up with all of these shenanigans. One thing was for certain, the next time I went fishing, I wore a life jacket just in case I ran out of faith.

All God wants is for us to be faithful to him. Let's go back to Job[4] and see what faith really means. Job's friends were convinced that he had done something wrong. Either he had sinned, failed to repent, was guilty of something, had been undermining religion, or was full of wickedness. They had all kinds of possible explanations for Job's "unjust" predicament. They even managed to shake Job to the extent that Job wanted a one on one conversation with God. As we saw earlier in Chapter 21 of this book, once God straightened Job out, reminding Job that it wasn't about him, Job repented.

Matthew reminds us that "faith the size of a mustard seed can move mountains"[5]; or as in John "uproot a mulberry tree and plant it in the sea"[6].

Jesus said; "the truth will set you free"[7]. Faith in Jesus means faith in truth. Faith in truth means faith in our God given abilities. Since I haven't seen mulberry trees planted in oceans or mountains moving very fast, the question is; what aspect of faith are we missing? There is more to faith than this humanistic aspect. God has given us many examples lest we say "I have done this". Gideon won a battle with 300 men that God chose[8] by the way they drank water; or Joshua defeating Jericho with walls that tumbled because of trumpets[9]. Where have we stored our faith? Is it in the correct place?

Joel Osteen in his book **"Your Best Life Now"**[10] encourages us to challenge our faith, test it, take it to different places. He contends that all of these trials improve our faith and that adversity builds spiritual character, spiritual quality, spiritual muscle, and spiritual experience. The "testing it" part seems to happen all of the time. Our earthly existence is a constant test of our faith in the promises of God. Some say that God tests us to keep our faith pointed in the right direction. Testing is welcomed according to Osteen because it helps our faith grow stronger. So don't be afraid to test it yourself.

I am reminded of Cloe, a dog at a fishing camp I have gone to for several years. The dog is permitted inside the main cabin where food is served, but she is not permitted in the kitchen where the food is prepared for obvious health reasons. On occasion, Cloe will sit at the kitchen door that leads from the serving area to the preparation area but will not cross the line. She will sit there in her best begging posture, but still will not enter the kitchen. Occasionally, the camp manager will call her trying to coax her into kitchen but to no avail. Even bribing her with food to come into the kitchen doesn't work. She has been trained not to enter and she won't. But that doesn't mean that she isn't tested. The camp manager tests her often just to be certain that she remains trained to stay out of the kitchen and she does.

Osteen indicated that no man can make you give up your faith and you can't give your faith to others. Each of us must arrive at our own understanding of faith. My experience is that each of us already has some faith but that all of us need to cultivate that faith so that it will sustain us in any given situation. Trust it to grow as we grow and develop understanding of how important that faith is.

God won't develop our faith for us. So our starting place is to have faith in our God given abilities. We can't just sit around waiting for our faith to kick in, but we can't rush it either. Otherwise we will most likely miss some important aspect of our faith understanding. We can't fight it either. We must let our understanding of faith develop at its own pace. Most of all, we can't dwell on the negative aspects we learn along the way. This means we must avoid the distractions that keep us from following the path God has given us. If we do, faith will take us to a new level of existence. It has been my experience that faith comes in cans. (Like "I can!")

Osteen also says that there are three kinds of faith. First, there is delivering faith. With this kind of faith, God turns situations around instantly. Secondly, there is sustaining faith, a faith greater than a delivering faith that has deep trust and belief in God that pulls us through anything. The third kind of faith Osteen professes is the faith that others have in us. He calls this faith a reverse faith.

Based on my experiences I would have to add one more kind of faith and that is the faith that God has in us. I call this a sustaining reverse faith. God knows what we can do even if we don't. Remember, God uses ordinary people to do extraordinary things. Just to name a few examples, think of Noah and the ark[11]; Moses and how he had to be convinced that he could lead the Israelites out of bondage[12]; and Joshua who had no idea how to capture Jericho and had to send in the spies[13].

God knows what each of us can do and individually, we know what we can do as well. God has faith that we will do our part, but He relies on us to take the first step. We have to have faith enough in our God given talents (and in the God given talents that we don't care to recognize at times) to do the tasks that God has set in front of us. God has never requested us to do something that we can't do. All of the resources we need for any God requested tasks are in our reach. God knows what we can do and like it or not, we know as well. We know what our God given talents are and we know where God wants us to be and what God wants us to do with those talents. Although we depend on our abilities, we need more that that because of our weakness. Faith in what God can do enables us beyond our weakness. What good is faith if we don't use it?

Another friend of mine, Dan Wolff, teaches what we use to call "manual arts" in high school. During the summer months, he had a roofing business to augment his income. He helped me put a new roof on my house one year. I suppose it would be more appropriate to say that I helped him. During the final stages of the roofing job, he asked me to apply some tar-like goop to various areas where sealing was required to prevent leaking. As I sat on the edge of the roof performing the requested task, I inquired how much of the goop I should use. His response was very useful. He said that the goop doesn't do any good in the can.

Faith doesn't do any good in the can either. I asked earlier, if you knew where you stored your faith. If your faith is in storage, you need to take it out and put it to use. After all, what good is faith if you don't use it? Remember, God is waiting for each of us to take the first step.

REFERENCES

1. *Following the Equator*, Pudd'nhead Wilson's Calendar
2. Matthew 6: 25-27
3. *The Real Princess (The Princess and the Pea)* by Hans Christian Andersen
4. The Book of Job in the Bible
5. Matthew 17: 20
6. John 17: 5
7. John 8:32
8. Judges 7:4-6
9. Joshua 6:1-5
10. *Your Best Life Now*, Joel Osteen published by Warner Faith Time Warner Book Group 1271 Avenue of the Americas New York, NY 10020
11. Genesis 6:9
12. Exodus 3
13. Joshua 2

DISCUSSION QUESTIONS

1. What do you have, by being faithful, that others might be missing?
2. What is one thing that has tested your faith?
3. How has your faith made you stronger?

THE FINAL SACRIFICE

CHAPTER 23

Did Mary Really Know The Little Lamb?
What Really Happened To The Flock?

What Adam and Eve had at the start,
Was love for God in their heart.

Much has happened since that fateful day when Eve encountered Snake. Still, God's purpose for mankind remains the same as it was before Eve bit the apple, worship Him and love one another. With all that we know about God, or at least all that we think we know, it is difficult to understand the concept that God wants us to worship Him. By that, I mean I have to question the idea that God would create a being for the sole purpose of having that being worshipping Him. What possibly could God gain from such a self-serving endeavor? My mind just isn't capable of wrapping around this notion. How could God, in all of His creation, hold Himself is such high esteem that he would create mankind so that He, God, could walk around showing off by having His man creature worshipping Him? This humanistic view conjures up some type of lackey attending to His every need, feeding Him peeled grapes, opening His car doors, announcing His presence, and whatever else our minds can imagine when we think about the concept of worshipping. I doubt very much that picture is what God intended. God has tried many ways to keep mankind attuned to His purpose. Worship Him!

By the same token, mankind has not been bashful about trying their very best to remain attuned to our own purpose. The world around us is what we see; what we "know"; and, probably, what we understand best or at least we think we understand. To most of us

God has always been and remains an enigma, and who can blame us? We don't encounter God in the same way we encounter each other. We don't know everything about God's creation. It doesn't take much for us to recognize that we are constantly learning new aspects about His creation. Take this computer tool, for example. All I have to do is highlight a word, hold the alt key, and left click and I can have access to a dictionary that defines the word for me[1]. Solomon tells us nothing is new here on earth[2]. In fact, Solomon claims, "Everything is useless, completely useless"[3]. He also questions the gains we make with all of our hard work[4].

On the other hand, Solomon might have a hard time today convincing most of us that nothing is new under the sun. Just thinking about my lifetime, we're no longer dependent on animal power for travel. Flying has become a convenient means of transportation as well. Who would have thought that we could be entertained with a talking picture in our homes? It wasn't too long ago that writing a document like this was restricted to just a few people and a printing press. I will bet that they didn't have to worry about loosing their documents to some electronic demon that decides to just shut down unexplainably.

From my viewpoint, everything is for nothing unless it is for everything and that means God. Now try and make sense out of that! I believe God deserves all of the recognition for His creation. There is nothing we can do without using God's creation. We can only create with what God has already created. The purpose for us to worship God is to remember who the real creator is. He doesn't want us to think we can exist on what we create. We were created to serve Him not for Him to serve us. He doesn't want us to think our creations were the result of our abilities alone. He doesn't want us to become so in love with ourselves that we overlook His part in our creations. We are only instruments in His universe; we are not the universe.

All of the challenges we experience in trying to understand our roles in God's creation can be related to our desire to realistically understand the difference between our perception of the world we live in and the world that God created. To overcome these difficulties, God simply wants us to "worship" Him. He wants us to give Him the credit for what He had created. For certain, He doesn't want us to be thinking that we have accomplished anything without Him. In that understanding, worshipping God becomes much easier. The awe that results from our accepting God as the creator is understandable. How could we possibly have done all that He has accomplished? He deserves our awe and our worship and He shouldn't have to ask for it. So what did we do to make Him remind us that His purpose for us is to worship Him?

Believe it or not, God understands our dilemma. In science, mankind has created equations that explain how different aspects of God's creation interact. In fact, mankind has even invented a term that accounts for those aspects in our equations that cannot be explained. The term is "entropy". "For a closed thermodynamic system, entropy is a quantitative measure of the amount of thermal energy not available to do work. Entropy is a measure of the disorder or randomness in a closed system. In the same sense then, entropy can be a measure of the loss of information in a transmitted message. All matter and energy in the universe has a tendency to evolve toward a state of inert uniformity. Entropy is also responsible for the inevitable and steady deterioration of a system or society"[5]. Basically, then, entropy represents what we don't understand about a given state of conditions where that state was explained to some degree of satisfaction.

In God's world, then, "entropy" would be that which we don't understand. If we could reduce God's creation to an equation, the entropy term would account for a huge portion in comparison to everything else that we think we "know" and "understand". When I think about the expansion of knowledge that mankind has experienced and the advances mankind has made reducing the unknown about God's creation to the known, I can't help but think about people like Galileo, Archimedes, Newton, Currie, Faraday, Bernoulli, Einstein, Pasteur, Salk, and many others. Of course, science is not all that it has been cracked up to be. Mark Twain once said, "There is something fascinating about science, one gets such wholesale returns of conjecture out of such a trifling investment in fact."[6]

Adam and Eve's world expanded suddenly once they understand good and evil. The entropy term for mankind in God's creation equation became a little smaller. However, in developing that understanding, God knew that He had a long road in front of Him before he could restore mankind to the desired state He originally had in mind; at least what I understand about what God had in mind. God knew that mankind with his newly obtained "free will" would have a hard lesson to learn and in order to learn that lesson, mankind's comprehension of God's creation would have to evolve from their perspective with significant assistance from the lessons that would result from needing to live with each other.

God trying to teach his man creation can be similar to parents teaching their children the hazards of playing in traffic. This teaching experience sometimes is frustrating. I know that at times the frustration is so extreme that we want to just tell our kids to go play in the traffic so that they can get the lesson over with. This reminds me of the lyrics from a song I heard from the Rush of Fools: "You are the only one that can undo what I have become"[7].

I don't know why we have such a hard time accepting the knowledge we learn from situations where we are not in control. Maybe "accepting" is too strong a word. The word "acknowledging" ought to work better. When I am teaching a new employee something new, I have found that the lesson is learned best when the employee needs the information to solve a problem. If I teach the lesson prematurely, I find that I have to teach it again when the employee is ready to learn the lesson. When I went to school, I expected to learn, but even then, the true meanings of the lessons was not realized until I encountered situations where the learned information was needed to understand some never encountered situation.

I am reminded of a favorite story of mine concerning payday and a bank. The story involves a man that wanted to cash his paycheck at the bank. Because it was payday, the lines were quite long at each teller. Finally, the man in my story reached a teller who asked him to sign the check on the back. The man refused to sign the check and the teller obviously refused to cash the check. So the man went into a second line where the same situation eventually occurred. This was repeated several times until the man arrived at a teller who was a little less patient. Although the man explained that he had refused to sign the back of the check to several tellers, this new teller was a little more forceful. He took out a baseball bat and hit the man on the head. Immediately following the head hit, the teller told the man to sign the check on the back. The man complied holding his head in obvious pain. On the way out of the bank rubbing the sore spot on his head, the man encountered the first teller who asked the man why he had signed the check for the last teller but wouldn't sign it for him. The man finally admitted that the last teller explained it better. Some times God just needs to get out His baseball bat.

Throughout the Old Testament, we find the prophets telling us that the reason God has done something was so that we would know He was God. For example:

""On that day," says the Lord, "I will cause every horse to panic and every rider to lose his nerve. I will watch over the people of Judah, but I will blind all the horses of their enemies. And the clans of Judah will say to themselves, 'The people of Jerusalem have found strength in the Lord of Heaven's Armies, their God.'"[8]

Just look at what He did for Adam and Eve. Throwing them out of the Garden and making them work for a living was designed to teach them a lesson about the "Who" that is in charge. The punishment was designed to teach them how good they had it. The lessons were designed to provide them an opportunity to learn at their own pace. Free will was God's opportunity for mankind to realize that God had a purpose, and that God had a plan, and that without God, mankind was nothing. God's lessons, however, required mankind to succumb to mankind's nastiest self before the lessons could be learned. Even then, God had to live with a multitude of generations who needed to learn these lessons over and over again. God had to live with His regrets as well. Just look at God's covenant with Noah:

"And when the LORD smelled the pleasing aroma, the LORD said in his heart, "I will never again curse the ground because of man, for the intention of man's heart is evil from his youth. Neither will I ever again strike down every living creature as I have done. While the earth remains, seedtime and harvest, cold and heat, summer and winter, day and night, shall not cease.".... "I have set my bow in the cloud, and it shall be a sign of the covenant between me and the earth.""[9]

Try as He might, His lessons only fell on a few ears that would listen. Despite signs like the "rainbow", disgust from God abounded. Pillars of salt, destructions of entire cities, even forty years wandering in the wilderness just a few miles from land he promised for a select group of people show us how disgusted he really was.

Was mankind ever going to be ready to learn these lessons? Snakes didn't do it. Knowledge of good and evil didn't do it. Living a hard life didn't do it. Being given a free will didn't do it. How much entropy must God take out of His equation before mankind learns that He is the Creator, the only Creator, and that nothing can happen without His input? Will there ever be a final solution to this age-old problem of ultimately learning the need to honor the true Creator?

He selected a group of people to show the rest of the world how living with Him was a good thing. Still, He had to send these chosen people into exile: to teach them that He was God; to teach them He was the only One they should worship; to teach them He was the only way to a full life; to teach them He was the creator, not them. Did they learn? Some of them did, but that still wasn't enough. A lasting and permanent lesson was still required. Mary had a little lamb all right, but what does that have to do with Adam and Eve and you and me?

REFERENCES

1. http://www.thefreedictionary.com
2. Ecclesiastes 1: v 2
3. Ecclesiastes 1: v 9
4. Ecclesiastes 1: v 3
5. http://www.thefreedictionary.com/entropy
6. "Life on the Mississippi" By Mark Twain (February, 1863)
7. Rush of Fools, "Undo"
8. Zechariah 12 vs. 4 – 5:
9. Genesis 8:22 – 21, and Genesis 9:13

DISCUSSION QUESTIONS

1. Why are lessons so hard to learn?
2. Do you worship GOD the way you want to, or the way GOD wants you to?
3. Does GOD deserve all your praise ?

THE FINAL SACRIFICE

CHAPTER 24

Can You Imagine Getting Up In The Morning With Nothing To Work For?

*What God had in mind at the start,
Was that humanity would serve Him from the heart.*

The snake sure divided humanity from God, or maybe, if you think about it, humanity divided themselves from God! In reality, though, God has not divided Himself from humanity. God has spent nearly 10,000 years, as far as we know, trying to determine how to convince humanity that He is the original creator, not humankind. All that God wants is for humankind to serve Him. Humanity's insistence on using God's creation for his own purposes seems more realistic to humankind, simply because humankind is more familiar with what they see and where they live.

Philosophically, humanity has tried to understand his existence since the beginning of time. In fact, how God fits into humanity's existence has become extremely mind bending. How humankind fits into God's existence has generated an enormous amount of consternation. No matter which way this controversy is considered, humankind would never be just lying around doing nothing. If the rest of humanity is anything like me, the wonder of existence would be challenging many thoughts. The very act of defining one's self is work. Take existentialism for example, this is a philosophy that emphasizes the uniqueness and isolation of one's experience in a hostile or indifferent universe. Existentialism regards humankind's existence as unexplainable, and stresses freedom of choice and responsibility as the consequences of one's acts[1]. The very act of humanity emphasizing his uniqueness and making his own self-defining choices[2] requires considerable thinking. And thinking requires significant work for most people.

Creation is more than a philosophy! Humanity has a purpose in creation and it is **not** a self serving existence for the individual. Philosophizing about why humanity is part of creation and why humans have set themselves apart from the creator only emphasizes how humans have "thought" that they can be like God. In the beginning, Adam and Eve had it made, but they still had much work ahead of them. In fact, the work that was required of them before they met Snake was probably the same work they had to perform after the snake intervened. The only difference was that if the work had been for God, it wouldn't have been hard. It would have been out of love for the Creator instead of out of love for themselves.

Humanity justifies what they do using who they are working for as the basis. As we all know, humans can justify anything. The problem is that justifying in the name of "good" can conveniently accommodate the "evil" that is in the actual intent. When it comes right down to it, the purity of the act is really known in the heart of the person performing the act. And, the real reality is that God can't be fooled. As the creator, He more than understands the motivation of any act. Reducing creation to what we can see, feel, smell, and hear belittles creation simply to accommodate themselves. Accepting the abilities of humanity as the limitation of humankind and not the limitations of God broadens the concept of creation. Humanity's abilities expand as they learn more about God's creation. Unfortunately, humankind's abilities also expand as they work to learn more about their abilities so many "think" they are creating. A more appropriate term for a human beings who think they are creating might be "uncoverer", since, in essence, everything has already been "created".

All that is, all that was, and all that is going to be, are only part of creation. Creation also includes love, emotions, insights, feelings, a conscience, and probably a few other aspects about being a human as well. Awareness of these more subtle parts of creation requires work to understand how humanity's actions impact the rest of creation. It would be "nice" if each of us as individuals was the only one that required consideration; such is not the case. Selfish gratification gets in the way of considering all creation and the consequence is that, often times, dire consequences are not considered until it is too late.

Maybe Adam and Eve "had it made" before the snake arrived, but did they have all of the other parts of creation like emotions, insights, feelings, and a conscience? They could have, either that or they learned them as the result of the snake encounter. Knowing the difference between good and evil and having a conscience that requires one to react to the difference between good and evil are probably two different aspects. The Adam and Eve story suggests that since knowledge of good and evil didn't exist before the encounter with Snake, they probably didn't need to have a conscience. This absence of a need for a conscience also suggests that all of those other touchy feely parts of creation didn't exist either. C. S. Lewis said that these aspects of creation have no survival value, but they give value to survival[3]. Lewis, however, used "friendship and philosophy and art" in place of the "touchy feely" aspects of creation. To survive, humankind was required to work hard whether they had a conscience or not. Survival without a conscience would be much simpler, just look around at the animal world. Humanity was created to be more than an animal. The result is that mankind needed to learn how to get along with others! We still haven't solved that problem yet!

Humanity is so blind that he cannot see that all inspiration comes from God! The "rebellious" nature of humankind must have been created in God's image. Humanity thinks they can create too, but doing it without God? Why does humankind think they can create without God? Kids rebel against authority to show their independence. So do humans. God has gone to great lengths for humans too establish a relationship with Him, but humans just do not seem to understand! The Old Testament repeatedly shows how easy it is for humankind to depart from a meaningful relationship with God. God really made developing a relationship with Him easy, but humanity insisted on going their own way. Following the Ten Commandments doesn't seem too difficult for the most part, at least on the surface; nevertheless, we humans lose patience and when we don't get our own way, we seem to find a means to achieve our desires and the first commandment, the most important commandment, is violated.

The most interesting aspect of all this give and take between God and humanity (or rather just "take" on humanity's part) is that humankind always seems to need to worship something. If worshipping God does not work out for him, he simply makes up a god that will not tell him he is wrong. Worshipping requires a personal commitment. Worshipping also means more than putting some object or person on a pedestal and bowing down to that object or person. Perhaps understanding what worshipping means would be helpful. The transitive form means:

1. To honor and love as a deity.
2. To regard with ardent or adoring esteem or devotion[4].

Perhaps the synonym, revere, would be even more appropriate. Even more perhaps devoted and upholding are works that should be used. Jesus made it simple "follow".

In the last chapter, being a lackey was suggested as a means of worshipping God. God does not need a lackey. As "The Creator," all of His needs have already been addressed except one. That one need is to be recognized as "The Creator."

The word "worship" probably confuses most people. Here is the deal—us humans are simply looking for the good life. We use our surroundings and what we know to accomplish that task. Worshipping means that we need to take time out from our quests to acknowledge the assistance that has been received. The root of that assistance, of course, is God The Creator. One of His commandments was to remember the Sabbath by keeping it holy[5]. Part of keeping the Sabbath holy means to take time to remind ourselves that all we have was created and that the creation came from God. Another part of keeping the Sabbath holy requires each of us to keep in mind that we are part of creation as well. All of these reminders must be taken beyond the Sabbath. True worship involves constantly remembering that we are part of creation and that creation is beyond all understanding. Humans can try as they might, but they will never create something from nothing as was done with creation in the first place.

The recognition of creation **requires** an **act** of gratitude that cannot be explained easily. This recognition requires humankind to acknowledge creation and their small part in that creation. This recognition requires humans to treat creation with a reverence that goes beyond individual needs. However, this recognition also includes accepting that individual needs are part of creation.

The awe with which humanity holds parts of creation is astounding! Just think about the sunrises and the sunsets and the stars and moon on a clear night. Although mankind is awestruck, consider how often we react to the need to "use" creation for our own purposes. The toughest part of acknowledging creation is accepting each other, using each other, and living with each other. For some reason, this part of worshipping creation becomes a competition for God's attention rather than a true worship experience.

Pastor Keith Foisy's sermon delivered 11/9/2008 made several points that can help with the development of a proper understanding of worship. One of those points concerns the tests and temptations we experience. This may seem to be a little confusing but as Pastor Keith explained both "test" and "temptation" have the same Greek root word. The word is peirosmos (noun) or peirozo (verb). So peiosmos (περοσμος) means testing or tempting depending on the context. Pastor Keith indicates that to "tempt" would desire failure. God does not tempt. To "test" would desire success. God does test. Keep in mind that humanity is not tested beyond what they can bear. We may think that the tests are sometimes cruel and unusual punishment, but in reality, the tests are temptations and temptations are tests. God wants us to Himself and He wants humanity to worship Him. The tests or the temptations, whichever way you want to consider them, are God's way to bring humanity back to Him. Actually, another point, God wants humanity to live in such a way that they don't need to be tempted. God wants humanity to always consider God as the creator and if we do, we won't find ourselves being tested. Evil is everything contrary to God's will. If us humans let evil tempt us, well, no wonder God reacts the way He does. We must learn to decide between ourselves and God. In so doing, however, other humans in creation can and do take exception. As a consequence mankind should prepare for persecution, but pray for deliverance.[6]

Worshipping God puts everything into perspective with respect to creation. Part of the worshipping process includes accepting the challenges (that the tests and temptations provide) as a sign that we have departed from the path that God wants us to follow. If we do not recognize that we have been challenged with a test or a temptation, it could mean that we have accepted creation for what it is and that we have our part of creation in proper perspective with respect to God the creator. It could also mean that ignorance is bliss!

The snake successfully tempted Adam and Eve. Why? God was testing them. Think about it! If their relationship with God had been one of accepting God as the Creator, one that permitted them to acknowledge God as the creator, and one that required them to humbly acknowledge that they were part of God's creation, God would not have needed to test them. Even more importantly, the test would never have occurred in the first place, simply because the temptation would have been meaningless. With faith and trust in God and His creation, Adam and Eve would have ignored Snake and God would not have had to teach them any more lessons.

Our worship gets us to that point where God doesn't need to test us and temptations are not valid. Worship puts our relationship with God in the right perspective. So what is the proper way to worship and what does living without temptation mean for God's relationship with humanity? We are about to find out!

REFERENCES

1. http://www.thefreedictionary.com/existentialism
2. Existentialism has its foundations in the thoughts of Soren Kierkegaard (1813- 55) and Friedrich Nietzsche (1844-1900) Kierkegaard is called "The Father of Existentialism". There are different forms of Existentialism: Theistic Existentialism v. Atheistic Existentialism for example. What Atheistic Existentialism concludes is far from Kierkegaard conclusions.
3. http://www.quotedb.com/quotes/359
4. http://www.thefreedictionary.com/worshipping
5. Exodus 20 v. 8
6. Keith Foisy is pastor of Evergreen Covenant Church, Branch, Michigan, starting February 2007 and was still pastor when this was written.

DISCUSSION QUESTIONS

1. Are we selfish people?
2. Does your conscience make you more, or less selfish?
3. Are you truly thankful, or just going through the motions?

THE FINAL SACRIFICE

CHAPTER 25

Who Needs Salvation Anyway?
We Have An Army For That Don't We?

God's message is something to yearn!
Yet, man is still struggling to learn.

Many questions were asked in the first few chapters. Perhaps two of the more interesting questions were "What was God thinking?" and "Without knowledge of good and evil, what is left, Blind Obedience?" Numerous topics have been explored in this book trying to expose or at least understand what it is that God wants from His creation. It is fair to say "Yes! What God wanted and still wants is obedience". But is it blind obedience? **NOT!** The obedience God wants does not need to be blind. He has done everything to make the choice ours. God wants us to experience all of His creation with our eyes wide open, not as blind beings without understanding. The truth about good and evil is that knowledge of the difference is the cause for us to separate ourselves from God. God has spent an eternity trying to show His man creation how to accept Him as the Creator.

In a recent sermon at our church, the pastor[1] stated that the first two chapters in Genesis were about creation and that the last book in the bible, Revelations, was about the end of creation. Everything else in the bible in between these two extremes is about how we can come back to God and how we can make things right with God. Having a right relationship with God has always been God's goal and He wants that goal fulfilled with our eyes wide open. From the very beginning immediately after Eve took that fateful bite, God knew man was going to be in for a tug of war with the devil. The main point in this sermon was taken from Genesis 3:15.

> And I will cause hostility between you and the woman,
> and between your offspring and her offspring.
> He will strike your head,
> and you will strike his heel.[2]

The point was that God had always planned for his man creation to experience hope for that right relationship. In these verses, God is promising mankind that an offspring of man at some future date would overcome the snake (the devil). Even in this promise, God is alerting mankind to the fact that the snake will also have an offspring that will "strike" the man's heel. The meaning of this hope is that mankind will have a means to overcome the evil that he encounters as a result of bowing to the temptation that the snake presented.

Isaiah 9: 6 – 7 actually tells us who this "offspring" will be:

> For a child is born to us,
> a son is given to us.
> The government will rest on his shoulders.
> And he will be called:
> Wonderful Counselor, Mighty God,
> Everlasting Father, Prince of Peace.
> His government and its peace
> will never end.
> He will rule with fairness and justice from the throne
> of his ancestor David
> for all eternity.
> The passionate commitment of the Lord of Heaven's
> Armies
> will make this happen![2]

It is time for a power check! Whose power do we live by, God's or man's. From the very beginning God only wanted his man creation, us, to have a right relationship with Him. He knew from the instant that man violated His trust, it would take a "God With Us" event to teach us all how to make that relationship work. We needed to learn this lesson on our own and we needed to learn this lesson many times. Just like the experience with the new employee told earlier in Chapter 23, learning when a lesson is needed creates the most lasting impression.

The lesson that God wanted to teach required a lesson that would be eternally remembered. In fact, the lesson involved eternal life. God feared joining the tree of life with the tree of knowledge of good and evil, Genesis 3: v 22: (The tree of life was the "other" tree in the middle of the Garden of Eden.[3])

"Then the Lord God said, "Look, the human beings have become like us, knowing both good and evil. What if they reach out, take fruit from the tree of life, and eat it? Then they will live forever!"[2]

Eternal life with knowledge of good and evil without God literally scared God. It scared him so much that He put guards on the Garden, Genesis 3: v 24:

"After sending them out, the Lord God stationed mighty cherubim to the east of the Garden of Eden. And he placed a flaming sword that flashed back and forth to guard the way to the tree of life.[2]

The arrival of the long foretold messiah was God's last measure to teach the lessons that were required for mankind to once again have the opportunity to experience eternal life. God never wanted mankind to go without having eternal life, but mankind insisted on thinking that they could exist without depending on God. Even when mankind was given opportunities to learn that their existence depended on God, they invariably resorted back to their old ways once they experienced just a little bit of independence. Misunderstanding, misinterpretation, and other convenient excuses seemingly always managed to cause backsliding and separation from God.

This final lesson had to be convincing! Saving His man creation from self destruction required an intervention that would remove all doubt that He was God! He was The Creator! He was the One to be worshipped! He was the One in control. He was the love that His man creation was seeking.

It is hard to imagine that God planned this from the beginning! It is hard to imagine that The Creator knew that His creation would not be convinced of His abilities until they were humbled into learning the lesson the hard way. It is hard to imagine that God knew that the curiosity He created in his man creation would separate mankind from Himself. It is hard to imagine that God knew that choice of good an evil would tempt mankind to think they could exist on his own. It is hard to imagine that mankind believes they can exist without God!!!!! That they can exist without God's creation!!!! That they can exist on the basis of what they think they have created without God!!!! The question has to be reversed! Humans, what are you thinking?

In order to deliver His final lesson, God knew He would have to come in person and "live amongst us." Coming as a superior being lording over his man creation was not going to cut it. Separating our understanding of our existence from understanding God, knowing God, and knowledge of God…. Wow! What an awesome task! No wonder God had to come in person to show mankind what was required. One important lesson that mankind forgot in all of this knowledge is that God does not forget. God's knowledge is the creation.

Looking back at the original sin of temptation (or disobedience), one question still remains. Why did Adam and Eve not ask for forgiveness? This lesson is probably the most important lesson and yet, it is probably the most important lesson that all of us fight <u>not</u> to learn as well. God knew He had to do something extraordinary to make certain this lesson would come through loud and clear; be experienced with meaning and with understanding and without the possibility of conveniently forgetting the lesson.

Learning that final lesson without the possibility of being subjected to interpretation or justification is another issue. The free will or free choice that God willingly gave mankind still leaves His man creation the opportunity to reject any lesson he wants. Putting words into God's mouth, "that is no longer His problem". He has provided all of the truth He needs to provide. He has given His man creation opportunities to right himself and will continue to do so without punishment. His grace goes beyond all understanding. That is because He is God and we are mankind. Mankind has not yet learned that creation is for all. No patents are involved. God knows that even with the best of lessons, the world He has created leaves mankind with choices and that these choices can be complicated. The complication comes from mankind not from God. Mankind cannot get away from confusing their needs with God's needs.

God's final lesson had to take on the image of man in order to be understood. The Son of God, the Son of David, the Son of man, the Messiah in order to be believed, understood, and accepted had to undergo many tests to prove he had the perfection required for this final lesson.

Surely, God agonized over this final lesson. He had to think long and hard about what it would take to convince mankind to take the right path: the path that would lead back to eternal life without involving evil. God simply would not accept evil in eternity. He proved that evil was not welcome in eternity with the guard He placed on the tree of life. He knew from the beginning that mankind's mind would be difficult to change once they found the "pleasures of evil". God knew that mankind would ignore good if it wasn't to his advantage. God had to question how He could convince humanity that their wicked ways were not in their best interest. Mankind's world was in the here and now; accepting a change that would give mankind eternity was a challenge indeed. Besides, mankind was already convinced that his evil ways could not earn themselves any brownie points with God. Mankind knew the difference between good and evil and they knew that God would not accept the evil part. God had a dilemma indeed! From God's perspective, it was simple. "Change your ways." A gracious God, He was willing to accept mankind's change without punishing them for doing the evil part. Proving that willingness would take some doing!

It is hard to imagine that this final lesson would have so many parts: proving that mankind can overcome temptation; proving that God loved His man creation no matter what he had done; proving that atonement for all of mankind's sins could be accomplished with a single lesson; proving that evil can be overcome with good; proving that good intentions are not enough to overcome evil; proving that purity of heart was a required necessity for God's purposes; proving that eternal life is worth all of the evil that exists; proving that God's love is already there and does not have to be earned; proving that our salvation from sin is secure.

An awesome God was required to accomplish this awesome task of proving the points in this lesson! He accomplished the lesson first with the miracle of an immaculate conception, then miracles of healing, miracles of restoration of life, miracles of using ordinary men to accomplish extraordinary tasks; and the miracle of using mankind themselves to spread the good news or better yet, to spread the news of good.

The final proof was that good could overcome evil even in death. Not only did God send His Son to show mankind how to live in accordance with His will, God also allowed mankind to kill His Son so that no more sacrifices would be necessary to atone for mankind's sins. God literally allowed His Son to go to hell for mankind[4]. As a consequence, just think, mankind doesn't have to go to hell, if he doesn't want to!!!![5]

Guess what, God is not done yet!

REFERENCES

1. Keith Foisy is pastor of Evergreen Covenant Church, Branch Michigan, starting February 2007 and was still pastor when this was written.
2. New Living Translation (NLT) Holy Bible. New Living Translation copyright © 1996, 2004 by Tyndale Charitable Trust
3. Genesis 2:9
4. 1Peter 3:1-20
5. Robert Schuler (Jr) sermon 3/16/2008

DISCUSSION QUESTIONS

1. Are your eyes wide open?
2. Can you exist without GOD? Really?
3. Is it time to change your ways?